MY FIRST
GOAL

MY FIRST GOAL

50 PLAYERS AND THE GOALS THAT MARKED
THE BEGINNING OF THEIR NHL CAREERS

MIKE BROPHY

McCLELLAND & STEWART

Library and Archives Canada Cataloguing in Publication

Brophy, Mike, 1957–
    My first goal : 50 players and the goal that marked the beginning of their NHL career / Mike Brophy.

ISBN 978-0-7710-1682-0

    1. National Hockey League—Biography. 2. National Hockey League—Miscellanea. I. Title.

GV848.5.A1B78 2011   796.962092'2   C2011-902130-7

We acknowledge the financial support of the Government of Canada through the Book Publishing Industry Development Program and that of the Government of Ontario through the Ontario Media Development Corporation's Ontario Book Initiative. We further acknowledge the support of the Canada Council for the Arts and the Ontario Arts Council for our publishing program.

Published simultaneously in the United States of America by McClelland & Stewart Ltd., P.O. Box 1030, Plattsburgh, New York 12901

Library of Congress Control Number: 2011925612

Cover art © Eric Pearle / Getty Images

Typeset in Palatino by M&S, Toronto
Printed and bound in Canada

This book was produced using recycled materials.

McClelland & Stewart Ltd.
75 Sherbourne Street
Toronto, Ontario
M5A 2P9
www.mcclelland.com

1 2 3 4 5   15 14 13 12 11

Previous page: Superstar Sidney Crosby holds the cherished puck from his first NHL goal. (Getty Images)

To my dear friend Al Chute, my musical soul mate. I miss you every day. Also to my cousin, Constable Bill Henshaw, a true hero if there ever was one!

I would like to thank Bob Waterman from the Elias Sports Bureau for his never-ending help; my agent, Arnold Gosewich, who made the project possible; Ralph Mellanby, a TV legend and friend; and finally, Lloyd Davis who once again saved the day.

CONTENTS

MY FIRST
GOAL

· FOREWORD ·

BY GLEN HANLON

LIKE SO MANY OTHERS, I had the good fortune to watch the mastery and majesty that was Wayne Gretzky's wonderful professional hockey career. You might say I had the ultimate front row seat. I certainly had the best seat in the house the night Gretzky scored his first NHL goal. That's because I was his first victim—the goaltender who allowed Wayne Gretzky's first NHL goal.

At the time—and for a long time afterwards, for that matter—the goal had no special significance to me. I was being paid to stop pucks for the Vancouver Canucks and one got by me. End of story. In fact, it wasn't until late in Wayne's record breaking career, when he was chasing down Gordie Howe's all-time goal-scoring record, that it came back to me with a vengeance. I was working with the Canucks as an assistant coach at the time and when we returned from a road trip I must have had 50 messages from reporters wanting to speak with me about being the goalie who allowed Wayne's first NHL goal.

Immediately my guard went up and truthfully, I didn't especially like to dwell on a goal I had allowed. It did, however, give me time to put things in perspective. We didn't go into the game against Gretzky and his Edmonton Oilers that night thinking this guy was a legend in the making. He was just a rookie. Not just any rookie, to be sure. But nobody had an idea that night of the heights he would hit in his illustrious career. Truthfully, there was a lot more pressure on Vancouver goalie Kirk McLean not to be the one who gave up Gretzky's record-setting goal when Wayne was going after Howe's record than there was on me that night.

Wayne was a phenom and there was a lot of hype surrounding his arrival to the NHL from the World Hockey Association, but there was as much talk about the exciting group of young players the Oilers had that year. Mark Messier and Kevin Lowe also joined the NHL that season. For my Vancouver Canucks it was just another game. It wasn't like we viewed this game any differently than any other game because it was going to have legendary consequences.

And yet it did. Over the years I have had plenty of opportunity to see that goal. It wasn't Wayne's first game, but it was so early in his career nobody really had a book on him. Nobody knew then how effective he would be operating from behind the net. Turns out the goal was typical for Wayne. He set up behind the net and got looking around. What would he do? When Wayne saw that the opportunity to step out was good he quickly darted to the front of the net and lifted a backhander past me on the short side. The way goaltenders dealt with that particular play back then is quite different than goalies do it today. You basically tried to poke check the puck away from guys who were coming out from behind. Now the goalies play a more upright style; they hug the goal post and it would be a lot more difficult for Wayne to score that goal. Then again, he's Wayne Gretzky; he would have found some other way to score.

I used to tell people I didn't allow that goal; Wayne scored it. To me there was a distinct difference. If you're part of history and you aren't on the winning end of it, you don't really like to talk about it. That's the competitive feeling that was inside me. But after you retire and move on with your life you come to realize it was a darn exciting experience to have been a part of. Of course I'm proud to have been on the same sheet of ice with the greatest player who ever played.

I wouldn't say I'm grateful to be the one who allowed Wayne Gretzky's first NHL goal. Probably a hundred other guys got their first NHL goals on me, too, but I wouldn't remember the other 99.

· INTRODUCTION ·

I WILL NEVER FORGET my first NHL goal.

Okay, it wasn't really an NHL goal . . . and, truth be told, it wasn't the type of goal I dreamed about when I would lay my head on my pillow every night when I was a kid.

But it was nearly an NHL goal—scored against an NHL goaltender!

It was 1973, and I was fourteen years old, playing house league hockey in my hometown of Burlington, Ontario. I received an invitation, along with a bunch of other house leaguers from various age groups, to play against some retired NHLers, the likes of Andy Bathgate, Bob Goldham, Pete Conacher, Sid Smith, Wally Stanowski, Ike Hildebrand, Cal Gardner, and Harry Watson. I was even named the starting centre, and just before the puck dropped, Bathgate looked down at me and said, "Get a haircut, kid." Apparently, my dad wasn't the only one who hated my shoulder-length locks.

There were about eight hundred fans in the stands at Burlington's Central Arena, and I was thrilled to see the puck coming free and right to me in a scramble in front of the NHL Oldtimers' net. Without hesitation, I snapped it into the cage. *Whoo-hoo!*

It has been said that a player never forgets his first NHL goal. That was the premise of this book when I set out to write it. However, I soon discovered that it isn't necessarily true. A couple of players I approached said with regret that they could not remember the circumstances of their first NHL goals. One is Peter Mahovlich, whom I included in the book in a chapter with his brother, Frank. Fortunately, Peter scored one of the most famous and memorable goals in hockey history, a short-handed tally in game two of the famous 1972 Summit Series, so I decided to keep him in the book.

When I first contacted Gordie Howe, he couldn't recall the details of his first goal. However, I remembered reading about it in a book at the local library and told Mr. Hockey I would check out the circumstances and get back to him. By the time I phoned Gordie back a few hours later, he had remembered everything about his first NHL goal. *Phew!*

Fortunately, most of the players I contacted about their first NHL goals were thrilled to take a trip down memory lane. For many, the excitement in their voices grew as they spoke about them.

I hope you enjoy reading this book nearly as much as I enjoyed writing it.

ONE

THE BEST OF THE BEST

Previous page: Wayne Gretzky scored his first NHL goal in 1979 and followed it with 893 over the next 21 seasons, making him the most prolific scorer of all time. (Manny Milan/SI)

BOBBY ORR

THERE HAVE BEEN MANY SUPERSTARS in the history of the National Hockey League, but when it comes down to the question of the best player ever, the debate generally centres around two players: Bobby Orr and Wayne Gretzky. And it's a close race, too.

Gretzky set just about every scoring record you could imagine in his illustrious twenty-year career and is the NHL's all-time leading scorer. He wasn't the fastest skater, nor the hardest shooter, but he had unimaginable vision on the ice, and nobody made players around him better than Number 99.

Orr, on the other hand, had a tragically short career—just nine full seasons. In the three ensuing campaigns, one with Boston and two with the Chicago Blackhawks, Orr played a total of thirty-six games. Knee injuries cut short what could have been one of the most amazing and productive careers ever. Still, the case could be made that nobody revolutionized the game to a greater extent than the shy young man from Parry Sound, Ontario.

In an era when most defencemen worried mostly about preventing the opposition from scoring, Orr wanted more from the game. Sure, he loved to shut down the other team's top players—that was his number-one priority. But it didn't mean he wasn't interested in joining the points party. When he got the puck, he didn't simply fire it off the boards or glass

5

and out of the zone. He looked for openings—like a football running back looking for daylight beyond his monstrous linemen as they cleared a path for his rush—and headed up the ice on a mission. His goal was to score—and if he could not do that himself, he aimed to at least help one of his teammates get on the board. The result was a new way of thinking for defencemen. Bobby Orr had been the sport's golden boy from the time he first joined the Oshawa Generals of the Ontario Hockey Association as a fourteen-year-old, so why wouldn't others follow his lead? Orr said nobody stood in his way when he started rushing the puck as a youngster. When he would gobble up the puck in his team's zone and turn up ice, fans would move to the edges of their seats. *What will he do? How far will he go?*

"I didn't have anybody who discouraged me from playing the way I played," he said. "Don't forget, they didn't have the draft the way they do today, so when I was playing in Oshawa, when I was fourteen, the coaches there were hired by the Bruins. They didn't discourage me or suggest I change my style. I just always played like that. Maybe it comes from playing river hockey or bay hockey. We scrimmaged . . . played shinny. That's how I learned to play.

"I actually started out as a right winger when I first started playing hockey, and I don't remember why I was moved back. But I guess it all worked out in the end. I believe it was Bucko McDonald who coached us in Parry Sound who moved me back to defence, but I don't recall why."

McDonald coached Orr during his peewee and bantam years. When Orr's dad, Doug, asked why he moved Bobby to the blue line, McDonald responded, "Bobby was born to play defence."

Truer words have never been spoken.

Being identified as an amazing hockey player at a young age can be a double-edged sword. For Orr, growing up in a small town in Northern Ontario, it meant having to move away from home at fourteen. Most parents won't let their fourteen-year-old sons walk to the bus stop on their own nowadays, but in 1962 it was different. His quest to play in the NHL meant leaving home.

It wasn't easy.

"I was so homesick," Orr said. "It was tough being away from my parents, my friends, but I understood it was the next step and I was looking forward to it, so even though a part of me wanted to go home, I just fought through it."

Orr joined the Oshawa Generals as a prodigy playing against young men up to five years his senior. Although he was baby-faced and looked every one of his fourteen years off the ice, Orr was an instant hero on it. He had 6 goals and 21 points that first year with Oshawa, and in his second season, at fifteen, he was third in team scoring with 29 goals and 72 points in 56 games. By now, the entire hockey world was aware of the young fearless defenceman who was changing the way the game was played.

In Orr's third season with Oshawa, he upped his numbers to 34 goals and 93 points, good for second on the team, and in his final season of junior he scored a whopping 38 goals and 94 points in 47 games—tops on the club. His 92 penalty minutes in his fourth season was a good indicator that he would not be pushed around.

"People ask me why I had the success I had in the game, and I think it really comes down to the love and passion I had for the game," Orr said. "Unfortunately, I think we suck the love and passion out of our kids by humiliating them for foolishness. I never had that taken out of me. It was never a job to me. It was never a big effort to go to practice. I couldn't wait to get on the bay or the river. When my turn came to play indoors, I couldn't wait to get to the rink to have some fun and be with my friends. It was a way of life, and I loved it. I was never told by my parents that I was going to be a pro hockey player and make money. I just had a great love and passion for the game and couldn't wait to get on the ice. I was one of the fortunate ones who got to the NHL."

As a youngster attending high school at R. S. McLaughlin Collegiate Vocational Institute, Orr proved he was more than a one-trick pony. Asked by the track and field coach if he'd be interested in running, Orr soon joined other runners for 7 a.m. training sessions. He found it pretty tiring to be getting home from road games in the wee hours of the morning and then having to get up to run through the halls at McLaughlin, so he packed it in.

"The coach then asked me if I could do anything else, so I tried my hand at javelin," Orr said.

How did that work out?

"I still hold the school record for longest throw," Orr said with a laugh.

After four years with the Generals, Orr was ready for the NHL. The Bruins held his rights, and boy, were they ever in need of an infusion of talent. Prior to his arrival, the Bruins had finished fifth out of six teams in 1965–66 and dead last the five seasons before that. Fans in Boston were aware of this teenage scoring phenom playing junior in Oshawa and couldn't wait to see him for themselves. Although the Bruins dipped back to last place in his first season, with a 17–43–10 record, there was no denying he was a special player.

Even though he missed nine games with a knee injury, Orr managed 13 goals and 41 points with 102 penalty minutes and won the Calder Trophy as the NHL's best rookie. New York Ranger veteran Harry Howell won the Norris Trophy as the league's top defenceman, and upon accepting the award, said he was happy to have won it that season because Orr would own the trophy in the years to come. Howell's off-the-cuff comment turned out to be quite prophetic, as Orr won the Norris Trophy in each of the next eight seasons.

In Orr's first game, on October 19, 1966, against the Detroit Red Wings, he didn't score, but he got to know first-hand why people respected and feared Mr. Hockey, Gordie Howe.

"I was watching a pretty pass that I made, and Gordie wanted to let the young player know the old guy was still around," Orr recalled. "He stepped into me, and I went down hard. That was my welcome to the NHL. I had my head down and the old fella nailed me."

Orr's most famous goal, without question, was his overtime Cup winner against the St. Louis Blues in 1970. Orr took a pass from teammate Derek Sanderson and skated to the front of the goal, depositing a shot behind Glenn Hall. As the puck went in, Blues defenceman Noel Picard tripped Orr, who went flying through the air, his arms raised over his head in celebration of his championship-clinching score. The picture of Orr flying through the air is one of the most famous and enduring images in the history of the sport.

Long before he scored that goal, however, it all got started with his first NHL marker, on October 22, 1966, at the legendary Montreal Forum. Orr managed the lone Boston goal against Gump Worsley in a 3–1 loss to the Habs.

"It was just a shot," Orr said. "It wasn't much of a big deal. It was a slapshot from the point that beat Gump. Hey, I think any time you experience a first it is a highlight, and scoring my first NHL goal was certainly a highlight for me.

I first realized my dream of playing in the NHL, and then I get my first goal. It was really exciting . . . a thrill."

When you consider all that Orr accomplished in his career, often playing hurt, one can only imagine what heights he might have soared to had he been healthy. The sport of hockey was robbed of so much more because of Orr's knee problems. Orr's first knee injury came in his rookie year and caused him to miss nine games. Each time he got hurt, doctors would cut into his knee and scrape away cartilage, until eventually it was bone on bone.

The Bruins won two Stanley Cups with Orr, in 1970 and 1972, and both times he was the Conn Smythe Trophy winner as the most valuable player in the playoffs. He was named the NHL's most valuable player in three consecutive seasons, from 1970 to 1972, and was the MVP of the 1976 Canada Cup despite the fact he played in the tournament while injured. Orr was inducted into the Hockey Hall of Fame in 1979.

Orr finished his career with Chicago after he was unable to come to a contract agreement with the Bruins. His first season with Chicago, he played in just 20 games, scoring 4 goals and 23 points. The next year, he had 2 goals and 4 points in 6 games, but his knee was so bad, he retired. Incredibly, Orr never cashed a paycheque from the Blackhawks, saying he was paid to play hockey, and if he wasn't playing, he wouldn't accept their money.

Through it all, Orr said he loved the game and loved playing. Even though there were huge expectations placed upon him at age eighteen, when he entered the NHL, Orr said he was never fazed by the responsibility.

"I never really felt a lot of pressure, if pressure is things bothering you," Orr said. "I didn't start to feel that until I couldn't do what I once did because of my legs. Then I started to worry, and I didn't feel good. Leading up to that, heck, I was doing what I always dreamed of doing and I was being paid to play a game. Come on, I had it made. I had such a love and passion for what I was doing. I was doing what I wanted to do; what I loved to do. I just wanted to go out every night and be the best player I could be."

And the best player Bobby Orr could be just might be the best of all time.

WAYNE GRETZKY

OCTOBER 20, 1978

NOBODY WILL EVER ACCUSE Wayne Gretzky of backing into his professional hockey career. Far from it.

Gretzky stepped into one of the most amazing professional athletic careers of all time through the front door and made the most of his exceptionally special gifts. He was a trailblazer who joined the World Hockey Association as a seventeen-year-old and then played in the NHL at eighteen. He became the highest goal scorer and point producer in NHL history, and left the game holding more records than any other player.

Gretzky—or the Great One, as he became known—scored from just about everywhere on the ice, and in every fashion imaginable. His first professional goal was scored for the Indianapolis Racers of the WHA, and his first NHL goal for the Edmonton Oilers.

"My dad always told me the backhand shot was an important part of the game," Gretzky said. "My first goal in the WHA came on a backhand. My first goal in the NHL was a backhand shot. The goal I scored to pass Gordie Howe's NHL record for most points was a backhander, and the final goal I scored in the NHL was off a backhand shot."

At the age of six, Gretzky began playing novice hockey in his hometown of Brantford, Ontario, skating against boys as much as four years older. As a ten-year-old, he scored 378 goals and 139 assists for 517 points. The kid with the white hockey gloves sure could score — and he hadn't even reached the peewee level yet.

Before he hit his teen years, Gretzky was a nationally known figure, and yet, because he was on the smallish side and was something of an awkward skater, there were those who suggested he'd never make it in the NHL—that he'd just be a flash in the pan. Even when he moved to Toronto to play Tier II Junior A hockey at fourteen and scored 27 goals and 60 points in 28 games, there were doubters. The next year, playing in the same league for the Seneca Nationals, he managed 36 goals and 72 points in 32 regular-season games, and then fired a whopping 40 goals and 75 points in 23 playoff games, but that wasn't enough to make him the top pick in that season's Ontario Major Junior Hockey League draft.

Incredibly, he was just the third player chosen, going to the Sault Ste. Marie Greyhounds, where, in his only year of major junior hockey, he led the league with 70 goals and 182 points in 64 games. By now, it was becoming obvious to anybody that there were no barriers Gretzky couldn't get past.

The problem was, Gretzky was too young to play in the NHL, which didn't draft players until they were twenty. While that would eventually change (players are now drafted at eighteen), Gretzky was clearly too good to continue playing against juniors, so he signed a seven-year personal-services contract for $1.75 million—a lot of money in those days—with Nelson Skalbania, owner of the WHA's Indianapolis Racers.

It was only then that Gretzky started once and for all to win over his critics. Even though he would play only one

season in the WHA—the last of the league's existence—
Gretzky made his mark.

"My first NHL goal was a big one, for sure, but so was
the first goal I scored in the WHA," Gretzky said. "I was only
seventeen years old and I wasn't very big. There were a lot
of people who didn't think I was ready to play at that level.
I wanted to prove I belonged.

"When I joined the WHA, I didn't really have a hard
shot, but I had a quick release. I decided that I needed to uti-
lize my backhand shot. My stick had a pretty straight blade
on it, so it was a lot easier for me to control where the backhand shot was going. It was a much bigger weapon for me
than it is for most players today."

Gretzky didn't score until his fourth game of the season
with Indianapolis, and he was relieved when he bagged that
first goal. It came in a 4–3 loss to the Edmonton Oilers on
October 20, 1978. Gretzky carried the puck into the Edmonton
zone on his own, and with three Oilers surrounding him in
the high slot area, he whipped a sudden backhand shot that
seemed to fool goaltender Dave Dryden.

"The thing I remember most about my first goal in the
WHA is the Oilers were the first team I'd ever played against
that matched lines," Gretzky said. "Glen Sather was their
coach, and he had Steve Carlson shadowing me. Everywhere
I went, there was Carlson. The funny thing is, we ended up
being teammates later in my career.

"I was driving into the offensive zone, and I just figured
I'd better get the puck to the net as soon as I could. I was a
little bit lucky on that one. It was a relief because . . . I was
really starting to feel some internal pressure before scoring
that goal. I had some self-doubt. Getting the goal eased the
pressure I was feeling."

Gretzky played four more games with the Racers and wound up with three goals and six points in eight games before his contract, along with those of forward Peter Driscoll and goalie Eddie Mio, was purchased by Oilers owner Peter Pocklington for $700,000. The teenage scoring whiz completed the year with 46 goals and 110 points in 80 games with the two teams.

After that season, the WHA folded and Gretzky and the Oilers joined the NHL. This time, he was an instant star, although he still suffered from insecurity. Gretzky's first NHL goal was another backhander that gave the Oilers a 4–4 tie, and it made him feel a little more at home in the greatest hockey league in the world.

"At that time, I was still fighting to belong in the National Hockey League," Gretzky said of his first NHL goal. "I was no different than any other eighteen-year-old. I was fighting to prove to people that I was capable of playing at that level. Even though I had a pretty good year in the WHA the year before, there were still lots of people who felt I still had to prove myself."

The funny thing is, Dave Dryden, the goalie he scored his first WHA goal against, was also involved in Gretzky's first NHL goal. With the Oilers trailing the Vancouver Canucks 4–3 in the dying moments of the game, Dryden was pulled from the Edmonton goal in favour of an extra attacker. Gretzky set up where he was most comfortable, behind the opposition's net, and when he got the puck, he fed it to his linemate Blair MacDonald in the far corner. MacDonald quickly passed it back to Gretzky, who took a step out to the front of the net and deposited it behind Canucks goalie Glen Hanlon.

"A couple of things I remember," Gretzky said. "Being an expansion team, we hadn't got off to a great start to the season. We played hard, but we weren't getting the results. We really wanted to win, or at least tie the game. It was late in the game, and I got the puck behind the net and I was thinking, 'I've got to get the puck to the front of the net.' I got a pass back from Blair, and I knew Hanlon was a left-handed goalie, so I tried to backhand the puck over his hand. I sort of missed the shot, and the puck went between his legs. The guys were joking with me in the locker room after the game that thirty years from now I'll describe it as an end-to-end rush with me splitting the defence to score, but that certainly wasn't the case. It was the first one and I was thrilled."

Gretzky finished his rookie campaign tied for the league lead in points with Marcel Dionne. Both players finished with 137 points, but Dionne was awarded the Art Ross Trophy as scoring champ because he had scored more goals, 53 to Gretzky's 51. And because he had played in the WHA the year before, Gretzky was not considered eligible for the rookie-of-the-year trophy, which went to defenceman Ray Bourque of the Boston Bruins. He was, however, the youngest player in league history to score 50 goals and was awarded the Hart Trophy as the NHL's most valuable player.

The goal against Vancouver and Hanlon was the first of the all-time record 894 goals he would score in the NHL, playing for the Oilers, Los Angeles Kings, St. Louis Blues, and New York Rangers, and was one of 2,857 points he would amass over his career. He scored another 122 goals and 382 points in 208 playoff games, winning four Stanley Cups, all with Edmonton. Gretzky's accomplishments are legendary. Aside from becoming the number-one spokesman for the game and paving the way for the game to hit new heights in popularity in the United States, Gretzky set or tied 61 records in his career, the most noteworthy being his career final numbers. There are other impressive marks, though, including most goals in a single season (92), most goals in a season including playoffs (100), and most assists in a season (163). In fact, those 163 helpers were more than Mario Lemieux, who finished second behind Gretzky in scoring, had in total points that year. Lemieux finished with 141 points, 74 behind Gretzky.

Over the years, Gretzky's work from behind the net became legendary. He was one of the most creative and insightful players ever to skate in the NHL. That area of the ice surface became known as "Gretzky's office." He said there is a very simple explanation for why he started to direct the action from that area.

"Back when I was a teenager, Phil Esposito was all the rage in the NHL, and the way he played, standing in the slot, was pretty much the way all centres tried to play," Gretzky said. "He was one of the bigger players in the NHL, and teams wanted a big centre in the slot, especially on the power play. I wasn't very big, so it didn't make a lot of sense for me to be in the slot.

"My coach in Junior B said that I should watch the way Bobby Clarke played for the Philadelphia Flyers. Clarke played behind the net, although more toward the corners as he tried to feed his wingers, Reggie Leach and Rick MacLeish. For a whole year, I studied the way Clarke played, and it was a big influence on how I ended up playing. So it's not like I got to the NHL and suddenly decided I was going to play behind the net. That was where I played and where I was most comfortable.

"Back in those days, as a defenceman you could physically knock guys over or push them from behind, and I didn't have the size to handle the pressure that the defence and even the forwards could put on me in the slot area.

By playing behind the net, I was sort of out of sight, out of mind. I utilized the net sort of as a decoy—almost as a pick. If a guy came one way, I could go out the other way. If he didn't chase me, I was just more patient back there. It was definitely new for the offence, but it was also new for the defence to figure out how to check that. Defencemen had been taught their whole lives to watch the guy in front of the net. It served a purpose for me, and in that era, it worked. I'm not sure how it would work in today's game, but in my era it was something that helped my career."

As did following his father's advice about working on his backhand shot.

SIDNEY CROSBY

OCTOBER 8, 2005

BY THE TIME SIDNEY CROSBY made it to the NHL, he was already a household name in Canada. That's not entirely uncommon for a player chosen first overall in the NHL entry draft, because Canadians generally eat, sleep, and breathe hockey. But Crosby is special. Like Wayne Gretzky, Mario Lemieux, and Eric Lindros before him, Sid the Kid was identified as a phenom in his early teens, and the media tracked his every movement. He even skated with Gretzky when he was just into his teens, and the Great One boldly suggested Sidney might be the player to break many of his NHL scoring records. That's pretty high praise from a player many consider to be the best that ever played in the NHL.

Unlike Lindros and Lemieux before him, Crosby—at five-foot-eleven and two hundred pounds—was not an overly big physical specimen, but he was a powerful skater with an unabashed determination to succeed. He had a magical combination of speed, grace, and undeniable toughness. Push him, and he pushed back twice as hard. Unlike some highly skilled players who like to hang around on the periphery, waiting for others to do the dirty work, Crosby's inclination was to get the puck himself and drive it to the net. Some wondered if he'd be able to play such a rambunctious style when he got to the NHL.

Not Crosby, though. He had big plans. Just seventeen years old, Crosby told *The Hockey News* in a quiet, but confident voice, "I don't just want to be the best player in the NHL; I want to be the best player in the world."

When Crosby's Rimouski Oceanic went to the Memorial Cup championship, representing the Quebec Major Junior Hockey League, he was front-page news across Canada. It just so happened to be the same year the NHL closed its doors to its players in a labour dispute, so junior hockey was suddenly the best game in town. If there were any questions about Crosby's durability, he cast them aside as he withstood an utter mugging night after night at the national championship in London, Ontario. It was shameful the way the officials allowed the best young player in the world to be slashed and punched—often after the whistle—game after game.

This was prior to the NHL's crackdown on obstruction, which has greatly influenced the way the game is played today at all levels of hockey. Hockey had become a rodeo on blades, with third- and fourth-liners interfering with the stars at every turn. A change in the way the rules were enforced, coupled with the arrival of Crosby, was like a double lottery win for the NHL.

Perhaps even more special was the fact that Mario Lemieux was back with the Penguins. Imagine the excitement to see one of the greatest players in history skating alongside the youngster many were calling the Next One!

"The fact he is here is a wonderful story," NHL commissioner Gary Bettman told the *Pittsburgh Post-Gazette*. "It revitalizes the franchise, and the fact Mario and the kid are together is a great story."

With the eyes of the hockey world upon him, Crosby failed to score in his first two NHL games. He had an assist in his debut on October 5, 2005, against the New Jersey Devils and followed that up with another helper against the Carolina Hurricanes two nights later. He managed six shots on goal in those two games, but couldn't find the back of the net.

"My very first shift in the NHL, I had a wide-open chance on Martin Brodeur and he stoned me," Crosby recalled. "I was all alone in front of the Devils net, nobody near me, and he made a great save. I wasn't really too upset for not scoring. I went to the bench and was laughing because I had just gotten stopped by Marty Brodeur. I wasn't mad or upset. I was just happy to be there."

Was he perhaps saving his best for his home debut on October 8, when the Boston Bruins came to Pittsburgh?

"By my third game, which was our first home game of the season, I was starting to feel a little bit of pressure," Crosby admitted. "I was thinking, 'I really need to put one in today.' I felt like I was playing pretty good, but I hadn't scored yet. Part of me, though, was still just happy to be there. I can't speak for other guys, but for me, I was just happy to be playing in the NHL and I was hoping my first goal would come soon."

With Bettman in attendance, Crosby did not disappoint the Penguins faithful. With 1:28 remaining in the second period and his team leading the Bruins 5–4, Crosby finally struck pay dirt.

"I was standing to the side of the goal, and the Bruins had Hannu Toivonen in net," Crosby said. "My linemate, Mark Recchi, was battling in front for the puck. Bruins defenceman Brian Leetch was tied up with Recchs, and Leetch accidentally poked the puck over to my side and I had a wide-open net. It was a tap-in."

Instant relief! The wait was over.

"When the puck went in, I was so excited," Crosby said. "It was like, 'Yeah! I'm playing in the NHL and I just scored my first goal!' It only happens once, so you try to soak it up. Everybody always remembers their first NHL goal."

Lemieux, who sadly only played twenty-six games that season before retiring once and for all, was thrilled to see his young teammate finally score the elusive first goal.

"It was nice to see him get that first one, which is always the toughest," Lemieux said. "The guys were waiting to see it and were really happy for him. It took a lot of pressure off him."

Unfortunately, the Penguins were unable to hold on to their two-goal lead and lost 7–6 to the Bruins in overtime, but Sidney, who also had two assists in the game, had his first NHL goal.

Crosby finished his rookie season with spectacular numbers—39 goals and 102 points in 81 games—but was not named the league's top rookie. The Calder Trophy instead went to Alexander Ovechkin of the Washington Capitals, while Crosby was named runner-up. Ovechkin, the first-overall pick in the 2004 NHL entry draft, had 52 goals and 106 points in 81 games.

Thus one of the greatest individual rivalries in NHL history was underway. Besides the Calder Trophy, Ovechkin won the Rocket Richard Trophy in 2007–08, leading the NHL with 65 goals; the Art Ross Trophy in 2007–08, leading the league with 112 points; and was named Hart Trophy winner as the league's most valuable player in 2007–08 and 2008–09. Crosby led the NHL in scoring in 2006–07 with 120 points and was the MVP in 2006–07.

There are a couple of things Crosby achieved, however, that Ovechkin is still aiming for: winning a Stanley Cup

(Crosby led the Penguins to the Stanley Cup in 2008–09) and an Olympic medal—Crosby scored the overtime goal that helped Canada defeat the United States 3–2 in the gold medal game of the 2010 Winter Olympics in Vancouver. A year after the Penguins were defeated in the Stanley Cup final in six games by the Detroit Red Wings, Pittsburgh turned the tables on Detroit, winning the championship series in seven games.

The Cup is every hockey player's ultimate goal, and an Olympic gold is a dream come true for many, but his first NHL goal is never to be forgotten.

PHIL ESPOSITO

JANUARY 25, 1964

"I'M HERE FOR A GOOD TIME, not a long time," may be an acceptable strategy if you are eighteen years old and partying it up in Daytona Beach during spring break. But if you are trying to launch a serious hockey career, then self-discipline is in order.

Phil Esposito liked to live in the moment. And it nearly cost him a glorious NHL career.

When he was eighteen years old, in 1960, Esposito had the good fortune to be invited to the training camp of the St. Catharines Teepees. A long shot to make the club in the first place because his skating was considered a little too slow for Junior A hockey, Esposito made up for his lack of speed and grace by having an undeniable nose for the net. Stick him in front of the net, get him the puck, and he was as good as goal—er, gold.

But when he wasn't on the ice scoring goals, Esposito admits he was on the lookout for a party.

"Everybody thought I couldn't skate well enough, which was true, but that wasn't the reason why I didn't make St. Catharines as an eighteen-year-old," Esposito said. "I actually made the team, but I got into trouble because I went across the river to Niagara Falls, New York, where eighteen-year-olds could drink, and I celebrated. I got caught. In those days, a manager could bury you for as long as he wanted. I was sent home, and I almost quit hockey."

After he was cut by St. Catharines, he was granted a tryout with the neighbouring Niagara Falls Flyers.

"I skated one lap around the ice when their coach, Hap Emms, called me over and said, 'If you couldn't make St. Catharines, what makes you think you could make our team?' He sent me off the ice."

The following season, Esposito was home in Sault Ste. Marie when he received a call from his pal, Angelo Bumbacco, telling him to get his butt down to St. Catharines. Bumbacco was a junior hockey player who would go on to coach the Sault Ste. Marie Greyhounds of the Ontario Hockey League in 1974–75 and was a fixture on the local hockey scene for years. The Teepees wanted him to try out for the team again.

"Angelo tells me Rudy Pilous, who owns the St. Catharines Teepees, wants me to come to try out for his team. I said, 'I'm almost nineteen and I don't want to lose the seniority I have in the steel plant.' He told me it was a rookie camp, and it was going to be held in August. I decided, 'What the heck, I'll go.'

"So I go to St. Catharines, and I'm having a good time. I never in my wildest dreams thought I'd make the team. I'm skating around the ice, and Pilous says, 'Hey you, fatso, come over here.' I skated over to him, and he asks, 'How much do you weigh?'

"'I weigh 215 pounds.'

"'That's too big. I want you down to two hundred pounds by October, and if you can do that, you come back and I'll give you $60 a week to play for us.'

"I went home to Sault Ste. Marie and told my mom, 'No more pasta.'

"I ate round steak, and that's about all I ate until I went back. It was cheap, and I enjoyed it. I went back to St. Catharines and weighed in at 201 pounds. Pilous said, 'I guess you didn't make it.'

"I said, 'What? Are you kidding me? Give me a chance.'

"Pilous said, 'Okay, you're on the team, but I'm taking $2.50 off your pay, so I'm giving you $57.50.'"

The steel mill's loss was hockey's gain.

Esposito wasn't an instant success with St. Catharines, but once he got rolling he wound up second in team scoring behind Ray Cullen, with 32 goals and 71 points in 49 games. The following year, he turned pro with the Syracuse/St. Louis Braves of the Eastern Pro Hockey League (they moved in mid-season) and continued his scoring exploits with 36 goals and 90 points in 71 games. The team remained in St. Louis the following year, but switched to the Central Pro Hockey League, and Esposito was ripping it up with 26 goals and 80 points in just 43 games when the Chicago Blackhawks came calling.

"I scored like crazy in St. Louis," Esposito said. "It wasn't my speed or anything else. I really focused on making sure I hit the net on every opportunity I had."

It was his ticket out of the minors. Although he didn't know it at the time, he was through with minor-league hockey. He was now an NHLer, and that was the way it would stay for eighteen seasons.

"My last game with the Braves was in St. Paul, Minnesota," Esposito said. "There was a big bench-clearing brawl, and I fought Tracy Pratt and got kicked out of the game. That night, I got a call from Gus Kyle who said, 'Phil, you have to get on a plane because the Chicago Blackhawks are calling you up and you have to be in Montreal to play against the Canadiens tomorrow night.'

"I met the team in Montreal, and I was thrilled. I sat on the bench for most of the game, until Chico Maki got a misconduct. Then I played two or three shifts. My first shift, I had to take the faceoff against Jean Beliveau, and I nearly crapped my pants. It was like, 'Wow, Jean Beliveau!' He was an idol of mine. He was big and strong, and even though he didn't look like he was moving very fast, just try to keep up with him. Forget about it."

Esposito's first NHL goal came in his fourth game, against the Detroit Red Wings.

"In warmup I was skating around, and I happened to noticed Detroit's goaltender, Terry Sawchuk, kept going down on his right knee when he was saving the puck. The first period, I didn't play a shift, but in the second period I was sent out with Bobby Hull and Reggie Fleming. We have a breakout from our own zone and I end up with the puck. I split the Detroit defence, and I have a breakaway from their blue line in. I give Sawchuk a little fake, and he goes down on his right knee, so I fire it up over his right shoulder."

Strangely enough, it wasn't Esposito's first goal that was his most lasting memory of the game. It was, rather, a run in with Mr. Hockey, Gordie Howe.

"After I had scored, I'm out there again, and our coach, Billy Reay, says, 'Let Bobby take the faceoff.' So I move to the wing, and now I'm up against Gordie Howe and Ted Lindsay while Hull takes the faceoff. All these Hall of Famers are out there. Bobby looks over to me and says, 'Have you got that old bastard?' Bobby and Gordie smile at each other. The puck drops, and Gordie immediately gives me an elbow right in the mouth. I could feel the blood right away. I turned around and said, 'You old son of a bitch,' and I swung my stick at him. Back in those days, you'd swing your stick at the pads down by the hips.

"I leaned over to Gordie and said, 'You used to be my goddamn idol!'

"'What did you say, kid?' Howe said.

"Quickly, I said, 'Uh, nothing, Mr. Howe.'

"Gordie and I became friends after that. He told me there wasn't a guy in the league that he didn't test when they first came in. He said if they didn't respond, he owned them for as long as they played."

Once Esposito finally got his priorities straight, or perhaps became better at sneaking out at night and not getting caught, he went on to become one of the most prolific scorers in NHL history. Esposito took scoring to new heights, becoming the first NHL player to crack the 100-point barrier, in 1968–69, and led the Boston Bruins to two Stanley Cup championships. In an era when scoring 50 goals was considered a monstrous achievement, Esposito scored 76 in 1970–71, and followed that breakthrough year with seasons of 66, 55, 68, and 61 goals.

At six-foot-one and 205 pounds, Esposito was actually one of the bigger players in the NHL in his prime. Today, he would simply be an average-sized forward. A laborious skater, he would plow his way to the front of the net and set up shop in the slot area, eight to ten feet in front of the goaltender. He was big and strong enough to hold his ground as defencemen tried unsuccessfully to move him. When he got the puck, he was a master of controlling it until he worked himself into position to take a shot. And unlike today, when players routinely take shifts that last between forty-five and sixty seconds, Esposito would routinely stay out for ninety seconds to two minutes, especially if his team was on the power play.

Esposito was part of two of the biggest trades in NHL history, first being sent to the Boston Bruins along with Fred Stanfield and Ken Hodge for Pit Martin, Jack Norris, and Gilles Marotte, and later being dealt to the New York Rangers along with Carol Vadnais for Brad Park, Jean Ratelle, and Joe Zanussi.

However, even though Esposito led the Bruins to the Stanley Cup in 1969–70 and 1971–72, he is best known for his all-world performance leading Canada to victory in the famous 1972 Summit Series against the Soviet Union. The Canadian players thought the series would be a cakewalk and were stunned to find out the Soviet players were not only on par in terms of their skill level, but were dedicated athletes in tip-top condition.

From the opening faceoff of game one in Montreal, it was evident that Team Canada thought it would be an easy night. In fact, when the left-shooting Esposito broke toward the Soviet net, he switched hands and shot right. It was his way of mocking the visitors. After being blown out 7–3 in the series opener, the Canadian players took things a lot more seriously.

Although Paul Henderson scored the game-winning goals in the final three games of the series, it was Esposito who was Canada's leader and best player. When the team fell behind in the series, mainly because they were cocky and out of shape, it was Esposito who pleaded with Canadian hockey fans who booed the players in Vancouver to cut the team some slack.

Esposito arguably played the best hockey of his career in the final four games in Russia as Canada came back to beat the USSR with a 4–3–1 record. He was the top scorer in the tournament, with 7 goals and 13 points in 8 games.

Esposito may have been a Goodtime Charlie, but he remains one of the great point producers in the history of the NHL. Esposito led the league in scoring five times, and twice was named the NHL's most valuable player. He was named Canada's top athlete of the year in 1972, and when *The Hockey News* ranked the top 100 players of all time in 1998, Esposito was ranked eighteenth. Not bad for a guy who came close to working in a steel mill for the rest of his life.

• TWO •

FIRSTS

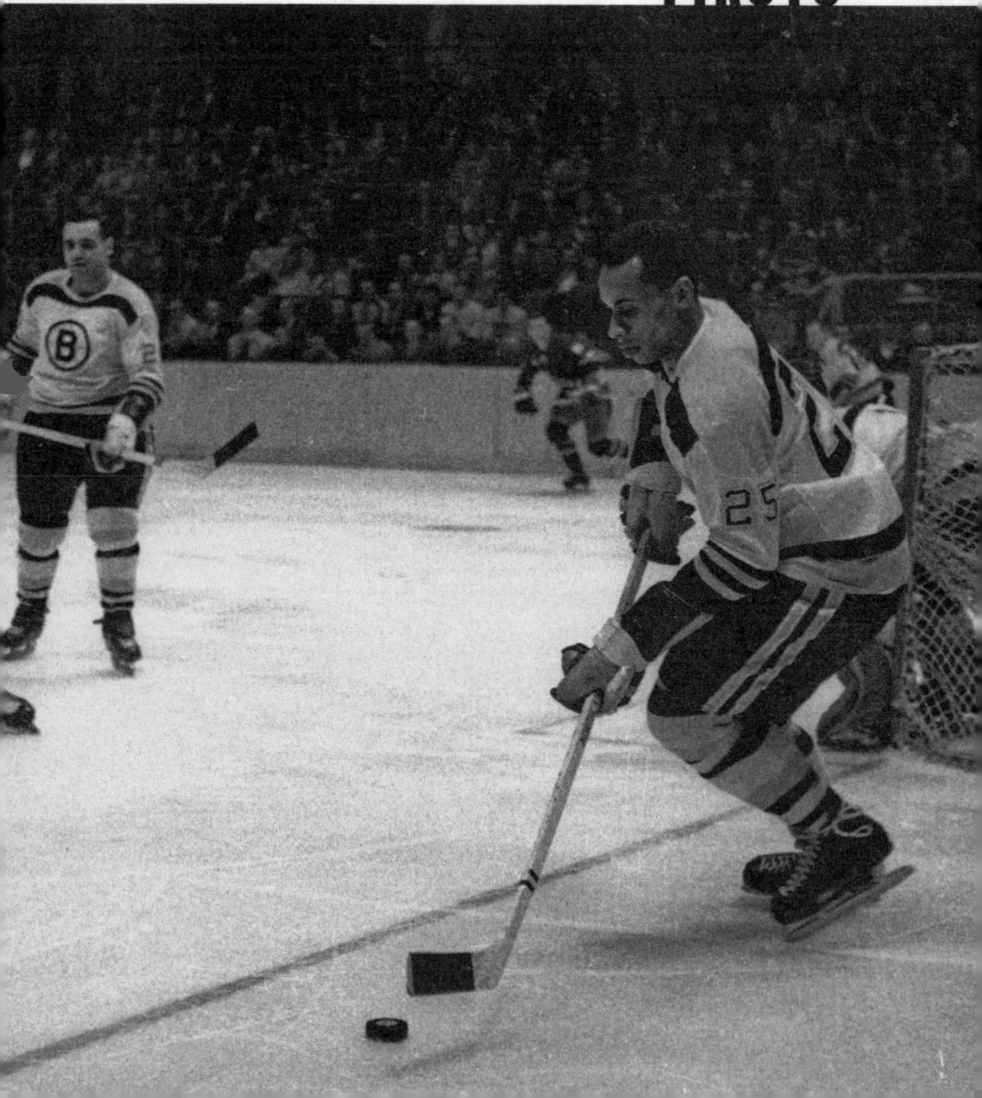

WILLIE O'REE

THE BIGGEST THRILL OF ALL was just getting there.

Although Willie O'Ree did not score a goal in his NHL debut on January 18, 1958, at the Montreal Forum, it was a monumental day in hockey history nevertheless. O'Ree, then twenty-three years old, broke the NHL's colour barrier, becoming the first black player to play in the league. Like Jackie Robinson, the first African-American baseball player to compete in the Major Leagues in 1947, O'Ree got there on his talent alone. O'Ree's accomplishment didn't get nearly the publicity that Robinson's playing with the Brooklyn Dodgers did, but it was a colossal accomplishment nevertheless.

When the Boston Bruins summoned the Fredericton, New Brunswick, native from the Quebec Aces of the American Hockey League, it was for one reason and one reason alone: to make them a better hockey team.

"I'll never forget my first game," said O'Ree after helping the Bruins defeat the Montreal Canadiens 3–0. "It was the greatest thrill of my life, I believe. I'll always remember this day."

Following the game, O'Ree was interviewed by Gordon Sinclair Jr. of CFCF Radio. O'Ree admitted he was pretty nervous in the first period; however, as the game progressed, he became more comfortable.

Playing on a line with Jerry Toppazzini and Don McKenney, O'Ree played his typical solid two-way game, using his speed and creativity to generate scoring chances for the Bruins. Following the game, he expressed frustration at missing on one particular scoring opportunity.

"I got the puck and I should have shot," O'Ree said. "I hesitated. I wanted to make a shift, and just as I did, I was hooked. But I should have shot."

Some fifty years later, O'Ree recalled his first trip to the NHL as if it were just yesterday.

"I had a couple of chances, but Jacques Plante came up with some good saves," he said. "The next day, we played in Boston, and again I had a couple of chances, but didn't score. I worked hard to get my first goal in those games, but it wasn't to come until the next time I was called up."

What was most remarkable was the fact that O'Ree had been struck by a puck during the 1955–56 season while playing for the Kitchener-Waterloo Canucks, and was 95 per cent blind in his right eye. That should have kept him out of the NHL, but he wisely kept his disability to himself.

The five-foot-ten, 180-pound winger proved beyond reason he could skate at the NHL level in his two games that season, but regardless, he was sent back to the minors, where he would stay for the next two years—first with the Aces, and the following year with the Kingston Frontenacs of the Eastern Professional Hockey League.

Coming off a fabulous season with Kingston, during which he scored 21 goals and 46 points in 50 games, O'Ree was once again summoned to the NHL by the Bruins in December of 1960. This time, he was up to stay—for the rest of the season, that is. NHL fans got to see what those who had followed O'Ree in the minors already knew: he was a gifted skater who didn't go looking for trouble, but wasn't one to shy away from it, either.

And this time, O'Ree finally scored his first NHL goal.

"It was in Boston against Montreal . . . New Year's night, 1961," O'Ree said. "I was playing left wing that night, and we were leading the Canadiens 2–1 in the third period. Both teams were down a man because of penalties, so we were playing four on four. I broke away from my check, and I was busting down the left wing when Leo Boivin hit me with just a perfect pass. I didn't have to break stride, and I had the after-burners on. I went into the Montreal end and skated past their defencemen, Tom Johnson and Jean-Guy Talbot. Plante was injured and Charlie Hodge was in the net that night."

For a moment, time stood still for O'Ree, who quickly instantly flashed back to some friendly advice he had received earlier in the evening from a teammate.

"As we were warming up, Bronco Horvath says to me, 'Willie, if you ever get in alone on Hodge, keep the puck low,'" O'Ree recalled. "'He's got a really good glove hand. Keep it away from his glove hand.' That really registered with me. As I'm breaking down the left wing and I'm all alone coming in on Hodge, the first thing that flashes through my mind is, 'Shoot low . . . keep the puck low.' I make a couple of moves on him, and I either shot the puck right along the ice or just barely off the ice. It hits the inside of the post and goes in the net. That made the score 3–1 for us, and then the Pocket Rocket (Henri Richard) scored [three] min-utes later. That made it 3–2 for us, and my goal turned out to be the game-winner."

O'Ree scored four goals in his 45-game NHL career, but the first one—obviously!—was special. Especially with the reaction it got from the Bruin faithful.

"The Boston Bruins fans gave me a two-minute standing ovation in the Boston Garden," he said. "I remember it like it was just yesterday. That made it so special for me. I dove into the back of the net and grabbed the puck and gave it to coach Milt Schmidt to hold onto for me. I only scored four goals in my NHL career, but the first one was the highlight of my life. The fact it turned out to be the game-winning goal made it that much more special for me."

O'Ree still has the treasured puck.

Unfortunately, the Bruins traded O'Ree the following season, to the Canadiens for Cliff Pennington and Terry Gray. The Canadiens were loaded with talent, and that, plus the fact that it was still just a six-team league, made it nearly impossible for O'Ree to get back to the NHL. Twelve games into the year, his contract was sold to the Los Angeles Blades of the Western Hockey League.

Sadly, O'Ree never made it back to the show, but he did enjoy a very good minor-league career until he retired following the 1978–79 season. In 1964–65, he led the WHL in goals, with 38 in 70 games.

Following his playing days, O'Ree worked as a supervisor for a company that looked after security for the San Diego Chargers of the National Football League, and in 1990 he began working for the International Hockey League's San Diego Gulls. In 1996, O'Ree was asked by the NHL to help run a hockey tournament featuring players from a number of urban hockey programs. It was here that O'Ree found his true calling. In 1998, he was appointed the director of youth hockey and ambassador for NHL Diversity, a job he still holds.

O'Ree was awarded the Order of Canada on April 7, 2010, another thrill of a lifetime.

"I was overwhelmed when they contacted me a little over a year ago, when my name was submitted," O'Ree said. "They said they would contact me later, and months went by before I heard from them again. It was so amazing when I was finally contacted. What made it especially great for me was the fact NHL commissioner Gary Bettman was on hand for the ceremony."

There will always be the debate as to whether the colour of his skin kept him out of the NHL beyond the forty-five games the Bruins gave him. Certainly, he played well enough in the best league in the world when given the opportunity. Regardless, O'Ree looks back on his time with the Bruins, and the fact he was the first black player to make it to the NHL, with special fondness.

"Besides breaking into the league on January 18, 1958, scoring my first goal was a major moment in my life," O'Ree said. "Sometimes, when they show game clips from my games with the Bruins, they show me coming in on Hodge and scoring my first goal, and it brings back good memories. I had that opportunity to score, and the puck went in the net. I just jumped for joy."

RON HEXTALL

"HE SHOOTS! HE SCORES!" has been a big part of the NHL lexicon since Foster Hewitt first coined the phrase. But "He saves! He scores!" has only been around since December 8, 1987. That was the day Ron Hextall of the Philadelphia Flyers became the first goaltender in NHL history to score a goal. That's right, actually *score* a goal.

Battlin' Billy Smith of the New York Islanders was *credited* with scoring a goal on November 28, 1979, but in truth he was only awarded the goal because he'd been the last member of the Islanders to touch the puck before Colorado Rockies defenceman Rob Ramage accidentally shot it into his own team's goal.

Hextall always had it in the back of his mind that he could score a goal if the right situation presented itself, and that's exactly what happened on that day in Philadelphia. With his Flyers leading the Boston Bruins 4–2 late in the game, Hextall looked down the ice, and there it was—an empty net. Boston had pulled its goaltender in favour of an extra skater.

Now all Hextall needed was the puck . . . and a little time and space.

With a faceoff at the Flyer blue line, you could see the nervous tension building from within Hextall, one of the league's most animated stoppers. He stood in his crease, alternately cracking the goalposts with the heel and shaft of his goal stick. The Bruins won the draw back to defenceman Ray Bourque, who sent it to fellow defenceman Gord Kluzak, who dumped the puck into the Flyers' end. Hextall tracked it down, and, standing to the right of his net, launched the puck down the ice. It was gobbled up by Bourque, who once again shot it back into the Flyers' zone. This time, Hextall got it and stepped to the left of his net. He calmly took aim, fired it over the heads of the skaters from both teams, and watched as it travelled two hundred feet and slid into the vacant Bruin goal. Teammate Derrick Smith immediately fished it out of the net to give to his goaltender for a souvenir.

In doing what had never been done before, Hextall made it look supremely easy. That's because he'd visualized doing it for years.

"There were times when people might have thought I was attempting to score because I was trying to get the puck out of our zone during a penalty kill, but that truly was the first time ever that I tried to score a goal," says Hextall, now the assistant vice-president and assistant general manager of the Los Angeles Kings. "The time was right, and it was the perfect opportunity. Kluzak put the puck right in my wheelhouse, to my left side, and I could see up ice and I knew there was no real danger of having the puck picked off. It was the first time I was really presented with that golden opportunity."

Hextall finished the season with a goal and 6 assists for 7 points, with 104 penalty minutes.

Just to prove the goal wasn't a fluke, Hextall scored another, this time during the playoffs—on April 11, 1989, against the Washington Capitals. Nine goalies have been credited with scoring a goal, but Hextall goes down in history as the first to turn the trick off his own shot. And he and

Martin Brodeur of the New Jersey Devils are the only goalies to have two goals in their careers.

While many goaltenders prefer to stay in their net and concentrate on stopping pucks, Hextall was always something of a wanderer. Maybe it's because his grandfather, father, and uncle were all forwards in the NHL. Bryan Hextall Sr. was a star with the New York Rangers from 1936 to 1948 and scored the Stanley Cup championship goal when the Rangers beat the Toronto Maple Leafs in 1940. He had 187 goals and 362 points in 449 games. Ron's dad, Bryan Jr., played 549 games with five teams, scoring 99 goals and 260 points with 738 penalty minutes from 1969 through 1976.

Uncle Dennis, the orneriest of the Hextall clan until Ron burst onto the NHL scene, had 153 goals and 503 points in 681 games with six teams in his big-league career, which spanned from 1967 to 1980.

Ron Hextall loved to leave his crease to chase down loose pucks as though he was his team's third defenceman. He also loved to get involved physically, and wasn't opposed to dropping his gloves to fight on occasion or to intimidate opponents by cracking them with his big goalie stick. In his final year of junior hockey with the Brandon Wheat Kings, he registered 8 assists and 117 penalty minutes.

Given the fact he was so active with the puck, it wasn't really much of a shock to him when he scored. Hextall says he didn't spend time in practice firing the puck the length of the ice in preparation for his first goal, but quickly adds that handling the puck was a day-to-day activity.

"I really enjoyed being on the ice for practice, and for that matter, before and after practice," he says. "I would play post-post-crossbar with my teammates after practice, where the last guy to hit the post or crossbar had to skate a lap of the rink. After a while, my shot became pretty good. I really loved handling the puck. I didn't necessarily practise to intentionally score a goal, but I did practise my shooting and moving the puck quite a bit."

And when he finally got his chance to score in a game, he didn't waste it.

"Honestly, the first thing going through my mind is the puck has to get out of the zone," Hextall says. "The last thing you want is to give the puck away and give the other team a scoring chance. After that, it was just a matter of crossing my fingers and hoping it hits the net.

"At the time, it was a little bit surreal. When it went in, my teammates all poured off the bench. I can remember a couple of guys screaming and yelling like we had just won a playoff series. It really turned into a neat thing, because the Flyers gave each player a gold-plated plaque with the game sheet on it. As much as I was the one who scored the goal, the neat thing was the guys telling me they were thrilled to be a part of history. It is an individual thing to score a goal, but when your teammates are so excited, that was more special to me than actually scoring the goal."

There were many things that defined Ron Hextall through his colourful thirteen-year NHL career, including competitiveness, feistiness, determination, and leadership. But in the end, the man who won the Conn Smythe Tropy as most valuable player in the 1986–87 playoffs and the Vezina Trophy the same season as the best goaltender in the NHL, will always be remembered for his scoring exploits, particularly his first goal.

FABIAN BRUNNSTROM

FABIAN BRUNNSTROM READILY ADMITS he wasn't too thrilled when he was informed he would watch the Dallas Stars' 2008–09 season opener—as well as game two of the schedule—from the press box. After all, Brunnstrom had been one of the most sought-after unrestricted free agents the previous summer, and the Stars had beaten out a number of suitors, including the Montreal Canadiens, Toronto Maple Leafs, Detroit Red Wings, Calgary Flames, and Anaheim Ducks, to secure his services. The Stars signed Brunnstrom to a two-year, $4.45-million contract, so it was expected he'd be an integral part of the team, and yet here he was, being asked to sit out and observe how the NHL game is played.

Dallas went hard after the twenty-three-year-old left winger because it didn't have a first-round pick in the 2008 NHL Entry Draft, having traded it to the Los Angeles Kings in exchange for veteran defenceman Mattias Norstrom. Consequently, they were forced to pay him big bucks, the equivalent of a second-round draft choice. So it was quite surprising when they chose to sit him for two games.

"It was frustrating, but our coach at the time, Dave Tippett, had a good talk with me and told me to just be patient," Brunnstrom says. "They didn't want to rush me into something they weren't sure I was ready for. He wanted me to sit in the press box and watch the first two games, and then I would play in the third game."

Did it help?

"It's hard to say," Brunnstrom says with a laugh. "To be honest, I don't think so."

You really can't blame Brunnstrom for that sentiment. No player likes to be a healthy scratch, especially when there was so much hype surrounding his signing with the team. If you ask the Stars, however, they may feel quite justified in what was certainly a controversial decision. Nobody knows for sure what Brunnstrom would have done had he played in the opening game of the season, but the results of his NHL debut in game three certainly speak volumes.

It's hard to say exactly how realistic the expectations for Brunnstrom were. He was joining the best league in the world from the Swedish Elite League, where he'd managed 9 goals and 28 assists for 37 points in 54 games playing for Farjestads BK the year before. Was it realistic to imagine that a player in his early twenties who had not been drafted had star potential? Was he a late bloomer—a diamond in the rough?

The Stars opened the season by losing 5–4 in overtime to the Columbus Blue Jackets and 3–1 to the Nashville Predators. With a return engagement set with the Predators four nights later, Brunnstrom was finally inserted into the lineup, as promised. He didn't disappoint.

"I remember I had in mind it would be really cool to score a goal," Brunnstrom says. "I wanted to play well, but I knew if I could score a goal, it would be amazing. When I scored that first goal, it was amazing. Then I scored another one, and then a third one."

With the game tied 2–2 in the second period, Brunnstrom put the Stars ahead at 11:45 with his first-ever NHL goal.

"Toby Petersen had the puck, and he made some good moves cutting into the Nashville zone on the right side," Brunnstrom recalls. "I was trying to crash the net, and he gave me a really good pass. All I had to do was put the puck in. It was a big relief. Like I said, before the game I was thinking to myself, if I could score a goal, it would be really nice. I was really happy."

He didn't stop there.

A few minutes later, after the Predators had tied to score, he notched his second of the game at 14:13, jamming in a rebound off a Brad Richards shot from a sharp angle at the side of the Nashville net. His shot beat Predators goaltender Dan Ellis on the short side.

Brunnstrom's hat-trick goal came late in the third period, when Richards, one of the most gifted passers in the NHL, was positioned behind the Nashville goal and spotted his new teammate working his way to the net. Despite the fact there were three Nashville defenders surrounding Brunnstrom, Richards made the perfect feed and Brunnstrom smacked it home for his third goal of the game.

Brunnstrom was completely unaware of the significance of scoring a hat trick in his first NHL game. It wasn't until he watched his third goal on the video display screen hanging above centre ice that he learned he was only the third player in NHL history to turn the trick. Alex Smart of the Montreal Canadiens was the first, scoring three goals in his debut on January 14, 1943, while Real Cloutier of the Quebec Nordiques did it October 10, 1979.

Afterwards, Brunnstrom met with the media and talked about his accomplishment. He was both shy and humble.

"I wanted to play and be part of the team," Brunnstrom said following the game. "I felt comfortable out there from the start. It was fun, but the most important thing was that we won the game."

Brunnstrom didn't have any family on hand to witness his amazing feat in person, and he didn't get the chance to call home to Sweden after the game because the Stars left immediately for a match in St. Louis the following night.

"The next day, though, when I turned my phone on, I had lots of texts from my family and friends," he says.

Believe it or not, Brunnstrom wasn't completely satisfied with the results of his first game. The reason why?

"You know, I actually scored a fourth goal, too," Brunnstrom says. "I took a rebound and the puck was loose. The ref didn't see it. I put it in the net at the same time that he blew the whistle. It should have been a good goal, but he disallowed it. It was a bad call. I should have scored four goals that night."

That would have been amazing.

Brunnstrom wound up with an impressive 17 goals and 12 assists for 29 points in 55 games in his rookie season, but dipped to 2 goals and 9 assists for 11 points in 44 games as a sophomore. He didn't exactly turn out to be a consistent scoring threat for the Stars. Nevertheless, Brunnstrom has fond memories of his first NHL game.

"Maybe it's a little bit different for Europeans than North Americans, but I dreamed about the NHL my whole life," Brunnstrom says. "It was always my goal to play in the NHL. You dream about playing your first game and scoring your first goal. That game is something I will remember for my whole life. For now, it's the best moment in my career."

JORDAN EBERLE

OCTOBER 7, 2010

THERE ARE FIRST NHL GOALS and then, well, there is Jordan Eberle's first NHL goal. Call it one for the ages. It was a goal any player who has ever played the game dreams of scoring.

Eberle was brought along slowly by the Edmonton Oilers, so this was a little payback for the team's strategy. Having scored 70 goals and 130 points in his first two years of major junior with the Regina Pats, there were those who believed the twenty-second-overall pick in the 2008 NHL Entry Draft was ready for the big league at age eighteen. However, the team was going through a transition after years of missing the playoffs, and new GM Steve Tambellini determined that the youngster shouldn't be exposed to some of the older and bitter players he hoped to clear out of the organization. He spent another year in Regina, scoring 35 goals and 74 points in 61 games.

Eberle attained international prominence in 2009, when he helped Team Canada capture a gold medal at the World Junior Hockey Championship in Ottawa, scoring an overtime goal in the semifinal to put Canada into the gold-medal game, and then producing the insurance marker in a decisive 5–1 win over Sweden for the championship.

"I think if you look at that tournament, most of the players that compete in it end up playing in the NHL. Obviously, as a

Canadian you are thinking about your team, and there's so much pressure on you to win it, for the most part you want to shine and do well, because it really can help you make a name for yourself."

When his junior season ended, the Oilers assigned him to play with the Springfield Falcons of the American Hockey League. It was a step up, playing against professionals for the first time, and he averaged a point per game with 3 goals and 6 assists in 9 games.

"I actually found it easier playing in the AHL than I did in the WHL," Eberle said. "You are playing with better players, and right at the get-go I had the opportunity to play with two very good players, Ryan Stone and Ryan Potulny."

The following season, Eberle was convinced he was ready to play in the NHL.

"I really felt I was going to make the team," Eberle said. "When I went to camp, I thought I played very well, and they told me I was one of the better forwards in camp. In the NHL, though, there's the business aspect of things, and with Edmonton's contract situation, it just wasn't possible for me to stay. The Oilers had too many players on guaranteed one-way contracts, so I was the odd man out. It was a disappointment to get sent down, but I didn't want to have that impact the way I was going to play. I wanted to prove them wrong."

The Oilers, however, had different ideas. The once-proud franchise had all but bottomed out. Many of the veterans who had helped the club make it to the Stanley Cup final in 2005–06, were miserable. Edmonton, because of the cold weather in the winter and the team's losing ways, had become one of the least desirable places to play in the NHL. Tambellini was determined to change the culture of the organization and didn't want Eberle to be around and get tainted during the transition.

Back to junior he went, and in 57 games with the Pats he scored 50 goals and 106 points and was named the Canadian Hockey League's player of the year. Other winners of the award include NHL superstars Sidney Crosby and Eric Lindros—who won it twice each—Mario Lemieux, Pat LaFontaine, Joe Sakic, and Dale Hawerchuk.

Further, he again played for Team Canada at the WJC, in Saskatoon and Regina. While Canada placed second, losing to the United States in overtime in the gold-medal game, Eberle managed 8 goals and 13 points in 6 games and was named most valuable player of the tournament. His 14 goals over two years made him Canada's highest goal scorer in tournament history.

"Obviously, I'm very proud of that," Eberle said. "If you look at some of the names of players who also scored a lot of goals at this tournament, it is very special."

Once again, when his season ended with Regina, he joined Springfield, where this time he scored 6 goals and 14 points in 11 games. Again, he was disappointed not to get the call from the Oilers, but his feelings were soothed when he got a call to play for Canada at the 2010 World Championship along with players from NHL teams that either didn't make the playoffs or had been eliminated from the first round.

"Playing in that tournament really gave me the confidence that I could play in the NHL," Eberle said.

During the summer, Tambellini succeeded in changing the makeup of his team's dressing room, making way for a new wave of talented youngsters that now included Eberle. Along with Taylor Hall, who was the first-overall pick in the 2010 NHL Entry Draft, as well as Magnus Paajarvi-Svensson (who shortened his surname to Paajarvi upon his arrival to the NHL), chosen tenth overall in 2009, the kids gave hope to a franchise that had been spinning its wheels. The arrival of the special threesome certainly could not be compared to the late seventies and early eighties, when Wayne Gretzky, Mark Messier, Jari Kurri, Grant Fuhr, Glenn Anderson, and Paul Coffey burst onto the scene, but for long-suffering Oiler fans, it was a step in the right direction.

Eberle, Hall, and Paajarvi had all enjoyed tremendous success leading up to their arrival in Edmonton. All that was left was to see whether the kids could succeed at the NHL level.

"I set my mentality in the summer that I was going to make the team, and hopefully, when I did, I would be ready," Eberle said. "That was my goal, and the fact that the three of us made the team took the pressure off us as individuals."

Eberle made an impact in his NHL debut on October 7, 2010, when the Oilers hosted their bitter rivals from down the road in Calgary in the first instalment of the Battle of Alberta for the 2010–11 season. It was a night hockey fans in Alberta, particularly Edmonton, had been waiting on for what seemed like an eternity. For Eberle, the wait seemed even longer.

And then it happened.

With the Flames on the power play and the Oilers leading 1–0 early in the third period, Calgary won a faceoff in the Edmonton zone and worked the puck to the goal, where goaltender Nikolai Khabibulin preserved his shutout with two good saves. Edmonton defenceman Jim Vandermeer retrieved the puck off a rebound and immediately turned up ice, where he spotted Eberle busting out of the Oiler zone. Vandermeer banked the puck gingerly off the boards, and Eberle retrieved in full flight about a foot inside the Calgary defensive zone.

Busting in off the right boards and racing at full speed, the right-shooting Eberle cut toward the net, but encountered Flames defenceman Ian White, who elected to try to halt his opponent's path to the net by sprawling on his tummy with his stick fully extended in front of him. This was White's attempt to knock the puck off the rushing Oiler's stick. Seeing this, Eberle quickly pulled the puck back and was in free. He dipped his shoulder with a quick faked forehand shot, drew the puck to his backhand, and, as he sliced past the goal, lifted a backhander high into the net past a startled Miikka Kiprusoff. It set off a roar inside Rexall Place that hadn't been matched in years.

"It was special," Eberle said. "Obviously, in your first game, you're a little bit nervous. My family lives in Calgary and some in Regina, and I had fifteen family members at the game, so I was pumped. It was a little nerve-racking at the beginning, but as the game went on, I really did soak up the atmosphere.

"On the goal, I saw White go down, and I don't know if it was instinct, but I pulled the puck back, and I think it kind of trickled over his stick a little, so I was a bit lucky. I got the puck to my backhand and made the shot. I had done that move before, and I knew it would work for me. It's really the only thing you can do in that situation, when the defence-man slides like that."

From the time Eberle got the puck until he raised it high into the Flames net for his first NHL goal, a mere two seconds had passed. And, without question, it was truly one of the most breathtaking first NHL goals of all-time.

"Hockey is a quick game, and you have to be able to think quickly," Eberle said. "Everyone remembers their first goal, and it is special, but to score a nice one is even that much more special."

To complete his magical evening, Eberle gained an assist on a goal by captain Shawn Horcoff when his shot bounced off the Edmonton centre's shin pads and past Kiprusoff. Eberle was named first star of the game.

Horcoff, who was energized by the arrival of the kids, was delighted that his new linemate had a successful debut.

"The fans came to see a glimpse of the future and they got it," he said.

For Eberle, getting a goal in his first game made his sometimes frustratingly slow path worthwhile.

"One thing I have learned from being a guy that scores goals is you don't really think about it when you're on the ice," he said. "It's when you get back to the bench that you kind of replay it in your mind. You wow yourself a little bit. The thing I remember is how the guys on the bench were every bit as excited for me as I was. That really made it special. It kind of showed me I was really a member of the team."

DEREK STEPAN

"KIDS DREAM ABOUT THAT. I never thought in a million years I'd be able to score three goals in my first game. It was really cool." So said Derek Stepan.

The six-foot, 182-pound centre from Hastings, Minnesota, played two years with Shattuck-St. Mary's High School, where Sidney Crosby, Zach Parise, and Jonathan Toews played before him, then spent two seasons with the University of Wisconsin Badgers. Stepan said the Shattuck-St. Mary's experience was one he'll never forget. No wonder: in two seasons, he scored 82 goals and 181 points in 123 games.

"It's a great environment," he said. "It's a small, little school, and everybody knows everybody. It's something that a lot of high school kids don't get the chance to experience. I can remember having classes with just ten kids, and seven of those guys played on the hockey team."

Stepan first gained international notoriety in the hockey world when he captained the United States to a gold medal at the 2010 World Junior Championship, played in Regina and Saskatoon. Stepan led the tournament in scoring with 4 goals and 14 points in 7 games. Considered a smart, responsible player who excels under pressure, Stepan decided to forgo his final two years at Wisconsin and turn pro with the New York Rangers, the same team that drafted his dad, Brad, in 1985.

Even after he was drafted, fifty-first overall in 2008, Stepan planned to do his four years at Wisconsin before turning pro. However, when the Rangers came calling in the summer of 2010, he changed his mind.

"I loved Wisconsin and had a great coaching staff and great teammates, so it wasn't an easy decision," Stepan said.

The Rangers were prepared for Stepan to start his pro career in the American Hockey League, but when veteran centre Vinny Prospal was injured prior to the start of the season, he made the team out of training camp.

"Every kid wants to make the team out of training camp, and that was the mindset I had, but in the back of my mind I knew if they felt I needed to start the year in Hartford [of the American Hockey League], that would be all right with me," he said. "My whole goal through everything was just to have fun with it. I get to play hockey for a living, which a lot of people wish they could do. I just tried to have fun and keep a smile on my face. The pre-season went well, and I was fortunate to make the team."

When he found out he was dressing for the Rangers' opening game, Stepan phoned his mom, Trish Coakley, who, along with her husband, Chris, made the twenty-eight-hour drive to Buffalo to watch her boy make his pro debut.

Stepan didn't exactly set the bar high when it came to his expectations for his NHL debut.

"I was just looking to play a solid game and just survive my first game without getting my head taken off or making too many mistakes," he said. "I was a little nervous going into the game, but I think that's natural for any athlete coming into any game. I get nervous before every game. I was really nervous for that first game, but a bunch of the players on the Rangers came up to me and tried to settle me down, which was nice. They told me to relax and realize it's really just another hockey game. They told me to try not to do too much; just go out and have fun."

Stepan said he had a tough time sleeping the night before the game, but when it came time for his afternoon pre-game nap, he crashed, which left him full of energy for the game.

The Rangers kicked off the 2010–11 season with a road game in Buffalo, and Stepan's first goal, which gave his team a 1–0 lead, came midway through the first period. Stepan played on a line with agitator Sean Avery and Ruslan Fedotenko.

"It was kind of a broken play, with the puck squirting back to our defenceman, Dan Girardi, at the right point," Stepan said. "Girardi took a wrist shot, and I got a stick on it, trying to get it to go toward the net because I knew it was going wide. After that, I didn't even know I had scored the goal. I thought Avery touched it, but when we got back to the bench, he told me the goal was mine. It was kind of a fluky one, but I guess that's how everyone gets their first one . . . off a shin pad or off a lucky bounce. I was kind of getting hit and I was facing the other way, so I never saw the puck go in. Even when I watched the replay on the bench, I thought it hit Aves. I still didn't know I scored it until they announced the goal, and then it was like, 'Wow, I scored.'"

In reality, after Stepan, who was positioned at the bottom of the faceoff circle, tipped the puck to the front of the goal, it banked off of the skate of Sabres defenceman Tyler Myers and into the net past goaltender Ryan Miller.

Stepan's magical evening continued in the second period, when he scored on a rebound at 15:08 to put his team ahead 3–1.

"I was on the forecheck, and the puck again went back to the point," he said. "I was behind their defenceman, and after Miller made the original save, the puck came to me and

I found a way to get it past him. It was a lucky bounce that came to me. At that point, I was kind of laughing."

Stepan completed his hat trick three minutes and twelve seconds later off a great feed from behind the net by Avery.

"Avery made an amazing behind-the-back pass to me when I was set up in front of the Buffalo net," Stepan said. "It went through their defenceman's legs, and the goalie was turned around, so I had the whole net to shoot at. At this point, it was like, 'Oh my goodness; I can't believe that just happened.'"

Stepan actually had a glorious opportunity to score a fourth goal, but he hit the goal post on a shot from centre after the Sabres had pulled their goalie in favour of an extra skater. When the game ended, with the Rangers winning 6–3, Stepan accepted a big hug from his mom and then quickly called his dad, who apparently, also has a sense of humour.

"My dad said to me, 'I wasn't watching the game—I was out and about. How did it go?'" Stepan said. "Of course, I knew right away he was kidding."

Stepan said he was the target of some good-natured ribbing from his teammates after he became the fourth player in NHL history to score three goals in his debut. Some joked in the dressing room about the NHL being too easy for him, and later, when the team was boarding the plane to return home, they continued to joke with him.

"I sat down, and a couple of guys walked past me and said, 'Wow, you've really changed since you scored those three goals; you think you're pretty cool,'" Stepan said with a laugh. "I was embarrassed."

Embarrassed, perhaps, but what a night!

JONATHAN TOEWS

OCTOBER 10, 2007

THERE IS NOTHING LIKE THE ANTICIPATION of your first NHL game, especially if you're a first-round draft choice and have been anointed as the saviour of a crippled organization.

Jonathan Toews, a six-foot-two, 210-pound native of Winnipeg, was the third-overall pick in the 2006 NHL Entry Draft, chosen by the Chicago Blackhawks after Erik Johnson went to St. Louis with the number-one pick and Jordan Staal went second to Pittsburgh. He was gearing himself up for the start of the 2007–08 season when a fluky injury occurred. In a move that can only be described as instinctive, Toews reached his hand out to block a shot during a pre-season game and wound up with a broken finger.

He knew right away it was a serious injury—so serious, in fact, it kept him out of his team's first two games of the regular season. Talk about a huge disappointment!

"I was pretty ticked off," Toews said. "I was maybe a little too emotional when it happened, but I guess that is to be expected when you have looked forward to making your NHL debut for so long. It was tough sitting on the sidelines for the home opener against the Detroit Red Wings. It was a pretty crazy crowd. Looking back, I realize it was pretty much a fifty-fifty split between Detroit fans and Chicago fans. That was the only reason the building was so full.

I was expecting the same thing for my first game, which was on a Wednesday against San Jose, but as it turned out, there were only about ten thousand fans in the stands. It really dropped off."

The Blackhawks, an Original Six team, had become an embarrassment to the league, but the arrival of Toews, along with winger Patrick Kane, offered some real hope for the future. Chicago hadn't won the Stanley Cup since 1961, the longest drought in the league, and even though there had been some good teams over the years, interest in the team was dwindling. In fact, in 2004, ESPN named the Chicago Blackhawks the worst organization in professional sports.

Late owner William Wirtz had alienated many fans by refusing to put home games on local television. However, when Wirtz passed away in 2007, his son Rocky took over the team and brought some more progressive ideas to the table, including televising home games and signing John McDonough as the team's new president. McDonough had been the highly successful president of baseball's Chicago Cubs.

Of course, none of that mattered if the Hawks didn't acquire some talent to play on the ice. The Hawks started the rebuilding by selecting Toews in 2006, and the following year they used the number-one-overall pick in the draft to get Patrick Kane, a shifty little right winger who led the Ontario Hockey League in scoring with 145 points despite playing in just 58 games with the London Knights.

Suddenly, Blackhawk fans had a reason to start following the team again, although it would take time for the building to be filled.

Toews came to Chicago with a very impressive pedigree. In 76 games with the North Dakota Fighting Sioux, he scored 40 goals and 85 points and was an impressive plus-38. Also, he helped Canada win a gold medal at the World Under-17 Championship and two golds at the World Junior Championship.

Toews also enjoyed one of the most dramatic individual performances ever at the 2007 WJC, when he scored three consecutive shootout goals against the United States in the semifinal, which enabled Canada to advance to the gold-medal game. Unlike the NHL, where players can only shoot once during the shootout, the WJC allowed players to take more than one shot. So after Toews scored his first goal, Team Canada decided to ride him until he ultimately won the game. It was a testament to his ability to play at a high level while under intense pressure.

His finger still quite sore, Toews made his debut with the Blackhawks on October 10 at home against the Sharks. He was definitely pumped for the game.

"I didn't expect to score on my first shot, but I really had a feeling I was going to get a break in my first game and find a way to score my first NHL goal," Toews said. "I took a pass from defenceman Brent Seabrook from the far blue line and chopped the puck past the defender, Matt Carle, which put me in alone on a breakaway. In a situation like that, you just have the feeling the puck is going to go in. And when it happened, it was amazing. It was such a great feeling to get the monkey off my back nice and early."

Indeed it was. Toews fired a laser to the top left corner of the net, past a startled Evgeni Nabokov to give Chicago a 1–0 lead at 13:43 of the opening frame.

"I was just trying to catch up to the puck," Toews said. "I knew the goalie, Nabokov, was deep in his net, and I figured since I was in tight, I had to go upstairs. It all worked out for me. I didn't really know how to react. I didn't give a big celebration or anything. I just went back to the bench and caught my breath. I couldn't really believe what had just happened."

Unfortunately for the Blackhawks, the Sharks came back to win the game 2–1.

Toews went on to have an amazing rookie season, leading all NHL freshmen with 24 goals and finishing third in points with 54 in 64 games. A knee injury suffered on January 1 kept him on the sidelines for 16 games and seriously hampered his ability to lead all rookies in scoring. Still, he was nominated for the Calder Trophy as the NHL's best rookie, but it went to Kane, who led all freshmen in scoring with 72 points.

Toews did make quite an impression on his organization, and the following year he was named team captain. At twenty years and seventy-three days, he became the third-youngest captain in NHL history. Only Sidney Crosby of the Pittsburgh Penguins and Vincent Lecavalier of the Tampa Bay Lightning were younger.

Often teased because of his staid personality, Toews has been dubbed Captain Serious and has been compared to Hall of Famer Steve Yzerman, who displayed a similar personality.

Toews' stock continued to rise after he scored 34 goals and 69 points in 82 games as a sophomore, and he was included on Canada's men's hockey team for the 2010 Winter Olympics. Playing with and against the best players in the world in Vancouver, Toews proved himself to be a worthy selection as he helped guide Team Canada to a gold medal, leading in scoring with eight points and being named best forward in the tournament.

If that's not enough, Toews returned to the Blackhawks following the Olympics and capped his miraculous season by leading Chicago to its first Stanley Cup in forty-nine years. Toews was particularly dominant through the first three rounds of the playoffs, and while he didn't score a goal in the final against the Philadelphia Flyers, he was named winner of the Conn Smythe Trophy as the most valuable player in the post-season. He was the first Blackhawk to win the award since it was originally handed out in 1965.

As for his first NHL goal, Toews says he still gets shivers when he thinks about it. He put the puck in a frame, along with a few pictures from his debut and the score sheet from the game.

"It's the one goal that really sinks in," he said. "It's your 'welcome to the NHL' moment. You know you have arrived, and if you keep doing the same things, maybe you can stay for a while."

THREE

O CAPTAIN! MY CAPTAIN!

Previous page: Hall of Famer and Maple Leafs captain Dave Keon slides one by arch-rival Montreal Canadiens. (Getty Images)

DAVE KEON

THERE WAS NEVER REALLY ANY DOUBT that Dave Keon would emerge as a star in the NHL, but like so many rookies before him, he had to wait his turn. Back when the five-foot-nine, 165-pounder from Rouyn-Noranda, Quebec, joined the Toronto Maple Leafs, rookies were routinely eased into the lineup while the veterans got the greater share of playing time.

Despite the fact he had been a star with the Toronto St. Michael's juniors the year before, leading the team with 33 goals and 71 points in just 47 games, Keon took a back seat when it came to his playing time with the Leafs. Quite honestly, it was what he expected.

"There wasn't a great turnover of players in the NHL when I broke in," Keon recalled. "I think the year I made the Leafs, there were only six new players in the league. The Leafs had two rookies . . . Bob Nevin and myself. It was pretty special for me. The Leafs had been to the Stanley Cup final two years in a row, so they were quite well established. I was going to hopefully make the team, and if I didn't, I hoped I'd play somewhere where I could get playing time and improve."

Unlike a lot of youngsters who join the NHL, Keon was already a gifted two-way player—a slick-skating speed-ster who understood the significance of playing solid defensive hockey. Many junior stars concentrate only on their offensive game. If an opponent had the puck, Keon was absolutely tenacious in his pursuit of getting it back for his team. That dogged determination would be his calling card in what unfolded as a spectacularly distinguished twenty-three-year professional career that would see him star in two leagues—the NHL and the World Hockey Association. A lot of kids made it to the big leagues based mostly on their ability to put the puck in the net, but Keon took great delight in shutting down the opposition's best players as well as producing for his own team. His resolve and refreshing attitude did not go unnoticed at his first NHL training camp in 1960.

"My training camp went very well," Keon said. "The first exhibition game I played was a 4–2 win over the New York Rangers, and I scored two goals. The next game was a loss against the Rangers, and I got an assist. Punch Imlach always told me I made the team in the pre-season. As I grew older and was one of the more experienced players on the Leafs, I would say to him, 'Why do I have to play pre-season games?' He would always remind me that I made the team in the pre-season."

Once the regular season started, Keon was relegated to part-time duty as Imlach leaned heavily on the players who had taken his team to the Stanley Cup final the previous two seasons, where they were beaten both times by the Montreal Canadiens. The Leafs were stacked with quality veterans, including the likes of Frank Mahovlich, Tim Horton, George Armstrong, Carl Brewer, Leonard "Red" Kelly, Allan Stanley, Dick Duff, and the venerable Johnny Bower in net.

Like most freshmen, Keon was expected to observe and learn, and, at the same time, be ready to hop over the boards to join the action at a moment's notice. For a guy who was used to driving the bus in junior, it was a bit frustrating being mostly a passenger in the NHL.

"The first two games, I barely got off the bench," Keon said. "I played two shifts in the first game, and maybe two or three shifts in the second game. The third game was in Detroit, and I hadn't played a single shift when suddenly there was a big free-for-all . . . a huge fight. Both teams were going to be two men short for what seemed like a week. Back then, when you were an extra player, you'd sit behind the door on the bench. All you did was work the door, with the other players coming in and going out. Up until the fight that night, that was my job.

"After a couple of shifts, Punch came down, tapped me on the back, and said, 'Okay, get out there.' I went out with Tim Horton and Allan Stanley to play three on three against the Red Wings. There was a faceoff in the Detroit zone, to Terry Sawchuk's left. I won the draw back to Horton, who took a shot that I deflected, and it went in. It was that simple. One minute, I'm sitting on the bench working the door, and the next minute, I have my first NHL goal. It was like, wow!

"I didn't see it go across the goal line, but I did see the red light come on, so I knew I had scored my first NHL goal. It was exciting. I remember thinking to myself, 'Maybe now I'll get some more ice time.'"

It was the first step on a path that would ultimately lead to legendary status for a man many believe is the greatest Maple Leaf of all time. It wasn't long before just about every young English-speaking boy who ever played street hockey would cry out, "I'm Dave Keon!" as the game began.

It didn't take Keon long to establish himself as a bona fide NHLer. With each passing game, Imlach leaned more and more on the twenty-year-old who repaid his coach nightly with tireless efforts and wound up with 20 goals—in an era when 20 goals was a momentous accomplishment— and 45 points in 70 games. In fact, Keon hit the 20-goal plateau in each of the first six years he played in the NHL.

Although Nevin—the Leafs' other rookie, who was twenty-two at the time—outscored him by 13 points, it was Keon who was awarded the Calder Trophy as the NHL's rookie of the year. Clearly, voters placed a high value on Keon's dependable two-way game.

From Day 1 in the NHL, Keon refused to sacrifice defence in an effort to score goals. He would never try to pad his stats if it meant putting his team in danger of being scored against. There was no cheating in his game.

"I knew how to get the puck when I didn't have it," Keon said. "That was my thing. I didn't wait for anybody else to help me. That was part of my training to be a complete hockey player."

The other thing about his game that made Keon stand out from most others was his ability to compete on a ferocious level without taking penalties. In his rookie season, Keon took just three minor penalties, for six minutes. In each of the next two seasons, he took just one minor penalty. Make no mistake about it: Keon was no shrinking violet. Nor was he a peripheral player, a guy who hung around the outskirts of the action and only joined the fray when it was convenient. He played the game hard and reaped the benefits, winning the Lady Byng Trophy as the NHL's most gentlemanly player twice, in 1961–62 and again the following season. Keon served as the Maple Leafs' captain from the 1969–70 season through the 1974–75 campaign.

When all was said and done, Keon concluded his career with just 117 penalty minutes in 1,296 NHL games with

Toronto and the Hartford Whalers, and 20 penalty minutes in 301 WHA games with the Minnesota Fighting Saints and New England Whalers.

"I knew what I was going to try to do, and I always felt that when you take penalties, a lot of times it is just being lazy, and I didn't ever want to be viewed as a lazy hockey player," Keon said. "You had to take the extra step rather than reach out for a guy with your stick, and not take any time off."

With that attitude as his driving force, Keon became one of the most lethal penalty killers the NHL has ever seen. In 1970–71, he set a league mark, scoring eight shorthanded goals. That was also the year he scored a single-season-high 38 goals. Coincidentally, on the night another future Leafs captain and legend, Darryl Sittler, scored his first NHL goal, in an 8–0 snuffing of the Detroit Red Wings, Keon was actually the star of the game, having scored two shorthanded tallies.

Keon finished with 396 goals and 986 points in the NHL and 102 goals and 291 points in the WHA. Perhaps his greatest achievement was being named winner of the Conn Smythe Trophy as the most valuable player in the NHL playoffs in 1967, the last time the Maple Leafs won the Stanley Cup. He was elected to the Hockey Hall of Fame in 1986, and twelve years later was ranked the sixty-ninth-best player of all time by *The Hockey News*.

Not bad for a guy who spent the better part of his first few NHL games opening and closing the door for the veterans.

DARRYL SITTLER

NOVEMBER 28, 1970

FIRST ROUND DRAFT CHOICES TODAY are generally afforded a certain amount of entitlement. Their place on the team is almost always assured, as is their opportunity to succeed early. It wasn't like that when Darryl Sittler was drafted by the Toronto Maple Leafs in 1970. The kid was a swift-skating stud in junior in the late sixties—a high-scoring centre with the London Knights who was being tabbed as a surefire NHLer. Problem was, the Leafs had a logjam at centre.

"I was a centre, and when I joined the Leafs, they had all kinds of centres," Sittler recalled. "They had guys there who were Hall of Famers. Dave Keon, who was still a star in the league; Norm Ullman, one of the best two-way centres in the NHL and another veteran; and even George Armstrong was still playing. They also had Mike Walton, Jim Harrison, me, and I was competing with another young centre, Brian Spencer. So it's not like I joined the Leafs and just stepped right into a spot that was waiting for me. I wound up playing mostly left wing the first few years, which was okay, but it wasn't the position I was accustomed to playing."

Sittler wasn't about to complain. He was just happy to be with the Toronto Maple Leafs. It sure beat the heck out of the alternative, which was playing in the minors.

Sittler was coming off a 42-goal, 90-point season (in 54 games) with the Knights in 1969–70 and had been chosen eighth overall in the NHL draft. That was the year the NHL expanded by two teams, adding Buffalo and Vancouver. The Sabres had the first pick and took Gilbert Perreault, while the Canucks countered with Dale Tallon. Looking back at the players who followed the top two and were chosen before Sittler—Reggie Leach, Rick MacLeish, Ray Martyniuk, Chuck Lefley, and Greg Polis—you could make the case the Leafs got the best player after Perreault. But even being a high pick didn't guarantee immediate employment in the NHL.

"Back then, whether you were a first-rounder or not, you generally spent some time in the minors," Sittler said. "It seemed to me like there was no question that I would be sent down after my first training camp. Still, I went to camp with the idea that I was going to work hard and make the team. That was my mindset. I was really determined to make the Leafs. I was in good shape and worked as hard as anybody else."

His hard work paid off, as Sittler impressed Leafs coach Johnny McLellan. Not only did Sittler make the Leafs, it was the start of a long and successful professional career that would never include a stop in the minors. If he had to skate on the left wing to play in the NHL, then so be it.

Oh, and if Sittler was feeling a little unloved because he was forced to play the wing, that feeling went away when he was given the number 27, which had previously belonged to superstar Frank Mahovlich. He had worn number 9 as a junior and figured management was sending him a message about where they hoped he'd wind up in the organization—as a star for the team.

Being just twenty years old on a team of mostly veteran players, Sittler felt it was important to be seen and not heard. That would change in later years, when he became the outspoken captain of the team and battled management and ownership over the treatment of the players, but for now, he was content to be a wallflower. He just wanted to fit in.

"I think I was the only single guy on the team," Sittler said. "Everybody else was married. I lived in Mississauga with my late wife Wendy's aunt, and my teammate Bill MacMillan and his wife lived across the street from us. The Hendersons, Paul and Eleanor, also lived out that way, and they brought me into their lives. Even though I was single, I was engaged to Wendy at the time. Looking back, I really appreciate the way the older players took an interest in me and looked out for me."

For the first couple of seasons with the Maple Leafs, Sittler had to bide his time.

"I was mostly a third- and fourth-liner, so I didn't get a lot of power-play time," Sittler said. "My big break came when a bunch of our players left to play in the World Hockey Association. That was in my third year."

In the meantime, however, he did manage to score that elusive first NHL goal. It didn't come as quickly as he'd hoped, but when it finally happened, Sittler was like any other kid whose dream had come true.

"It's interesting. It was in November against the Detroit Red Wings," Sittler said. "A few weeks had already gone by in the regular season, and I still hadn't scored a goal. That night, I did my very first interview, after the first period with Ward Cornell on *Hockey Night in Canada*, which was a thrill unto itself. I was kind of a shy and nervous kid back then. Ward said to me, 'You know, Darryl, we have had a few youngsters like yourself on before, and they have gone out and scored a goal after their interview.' Sure enough, I went out in the next period and scored my first NHL goal."

It was a very shy and humble Sittler who sat down with Cornell for his *Hockey Night in Canada* debut. Sittler talked about being switched to left wing from centre and about how veteran goaltender Jacques Plante had been key in helping him make the adjustment to professional hockey.

Strangely enough, when Sittler finally scored his first of 484 NHL goals, it was one of the guys who had been playing ahead of him at centre that lent him a helping hand.

"I was cutting through centre on a rush, and Mike Walton threw me a pass," Sittler said. "I carried it into the Detroit zone and used the defenceman as a bit of a screen as I took my shot. The shot came from between the hash marks. You have dreams of playing in the National Hockey League, and to score a goal is really putting your mark on the fact you scored while playing at the highest level of hockey in the world. Whether you score one goal, ten goals or five hundred goals, you always remember your first goal—that's for sure."

Sittler's first was also the first for an opponent.

"When I scored, I was brave enough to grab the puck because I was so excited and thrilled about it," Sittler said. "I didn't realize until after the fact that it was the first goal that Detroit's goalie, Don 'Smokey' McLeod, had allowed in the NHL. My first goal was the first he let in, but I got the puck."

Once Sittler was established as a bona fide top-line centre, he went on to have the splendid career that everybody forecast before he joined the NHL. As a player who combined great offensive skills as well as toughness, Sittler became one of the most popular players in Maple Leafs history. In 1,096 regular-season games, Sittler added 637 assists to go with his 484 goals, for 1,121 points. Few players can boast that they scored more than a point per game in the NHL. While he was not fortunate enough to win the Stanley Cup, Sitter was an excellent playoff performer, counting 29 goals and 74 points in 76 post-season games.

While many players hope and pray for one career-defining night, Sittler was blessed with three. On February 7, 1976, he became the first NHL player in history to record ten points in a game as the Maple Leafs defeated the Boston Bruins, 11–4. Sittler lit up Bruins goaltender Dave Reece for six goals and four assists, and following the game, in typical modest fashion, he told the *Toronto Sun*: "It was nice to get lucky, and it was sure nice to beat the Bruins, especially when you consider we've been struggling lately and they've played so well."

On April 22, Sittler enjoyed another golden moment when he exploded for five goals in a playoff game against the Philadelphia Flyers. Sittler continues to share the record for most goals in a playoff game with Newsy Lalonde, Maurice "Rocket" Richard, Reggie Leach, and Mario Lemieux.

Finally, that summer, Sittler was included on Team Canada for the inaugural Canada Cup. Canada was a powerhouse, but European teams had made great strides over the years, so this tournament was not going to be a cakewalk for the host country. For years, it had been Canada and the Soviet Union as the world's two hockey powers, but in this tournament Czechoslovakia made it to the final against Canada.

During the tournament, Team Canada assistant coach Don Cherry noticed that Czech goalie Vladimir Dzurilla would come way out of his net to challenge opposing shooters. Cherry reckoned that if a player got in alone on Dzurilla and faked a shot, he might be able to freeze the stopper, step around him, and fire into the vacated net.

That was exactly what was going through Sittler's mind in overtime of the championship game, when he broke in on the left side. He saw Dzurilla coming out at him, so he took Cherry's advice. When Dzurilla froze on the fake slapshot, Sittler merely moved to his left and shot the puck into the empty net.

Sittler was inducted into the Hockey Hall of Fame in 1989, and, following his career, has worked with the Maple Leafs as an ambassador.

To this day, Sittler insists a player's first NHL goal is special.

"I played with Dave Poulin in Philadelphia, and he now works in our [the Leafs'] organization," Sittler said. "I didn't realize until he told me that I assisted on his first NHL goal. I don't even recall that, but because it was his first NHL goal, he remembers it like it was yesterday. I also assisted on Ron Wilson's first goal in the NHL."

"That's true," Wilson—now the head coach of the Leafs—says. "Not only that, Darryl scored a goal on a pass that I gave to him on my first shift!"

DOUG GILMOUR

NOVEMBER 1, 1983

THERE ARE LITTLE HOCKEY PLAYERS, smallish guys who defy the odds by making it to the NHL. And then there is Doug Gilmour.

When Gilmour first joined the Cornwall Royals, who were in the Quebec Major Junior Hockey league at the time, he stood five-foot-nine and weighed, if you can believe it, 140 pounds. Not only that, he played defence!

They say good things come in small packages, but this was testing the boundaries of that theory. But as he would do throughout his amazing twenty-year NHL career, Gilmour not only ignored those who claimed he was too small, he went out of his way to prove he could play with the same ferociousness as a player twice his size.

"Truthfully, I didn't know I was small," Gilmour said. "When I put my equipment on, I know I looked small, but personally, I didn't feel like a small player. You're out there to play the game. In the back of your mind, there's always the fear of getting hurt, but once you stop thinking about that, you just go out and play. You're going to get hit, but you don't always feel it. Sometimes I did, because I didn't wear much equipment. You just try not to put yourself in a position to be hurt."

Although he had been cut numerous times from teams because coaches couldn't get past his lack of size, he never let that deter his goal of making it to the NHL. It was the size of his heart that was his driving force.

"My size was always an issue for others, but it wasn't for me," Gilmour said. "The one time that really stands out was when I was a defenceman, playing Junior B with the Kingston Voyageurs, and I was getting about three minutes of ice time a game as a sixteen-year-old. I asked for my release so I could go back and play major midget, but the Belleville Bulls, who were a Tier I team [a step above Junior B] called and wanted me to play for them. I started on defence with the Bulls, but in the playoffs we had some injuries and they moved me up to left wing. Cornwall drafted me and told me they wanted me to play forward. It was a good fit.

"When I was drafted to Cornwall, I'm certain not too many people believed I had a realistic chance to make the team. Obviously, I was an offensive defenceman, and they had a plan to move me up to forward. The first year, I broke my collarbone and we went to the Memorial Cup . . . it was a great year for the team. The following year, I had 119 points in the league and finished in the top ten in scoring in the league. I had been passed over in the NHL draft after my first year in the league, but after my second year, I was drafted in the seventh round by St. Louis. It was a little frustrating, having outscored guys who were being drafted in the first, second, and third rounds.

"My last year, I had a big year in junior, but still there was no contract waiting for me until mid-August."

"Big year" is an understatement. Gilmour put up mind-boggling numbers with the Royals: 70 goals and 177 points in 60 games in the regular season, to go with 8 goals and 18 points in 8 playoff games. And yet the Blues were not tripping over themselves to get his name on a contract. In fact, as the summer progressed, Gilmour had to look for other options and settled on Düsseldorf, Germany.

The Blues were owned by Ralston Purina at the time Gilmour was drafted, but were sold to Harry Ornest in the summer of 1983 after Gilmour had graduated from junior. Ron Caron was signed as the team's new general manager, and he put the word out, through Gilmour's agent, Larry Kelly, that he wanted to sign the tiny scoring ace. The team's coach, Jacques Demers, had no issue with Gilmour's size, but felt the team had enough scoring up front and asked Gilmour to be his checking centre.

"It was great news for me," Gilmour said. "I had been in Germany for seven or eight days, and they were getting ready to start their season. That's when Larry Kelly told me to get on a plane and come home—I wasn't going to sign there. I went to St. Louis and met Jacques, and he took a look at me and shook his head. I think I was around five-foot-nine and maybe 160 pounds. He knew my stats, but didn't know me as a player. We had Blake Dunlop, Bernie Federko, Mike Zuke, Larry Patey, Alain Lemieux, and they signed Guy Chouinard, so they had the offensive experience. Jacques basically said, 'If you want to make this hockey club, you have to check . . . can you check?' I said, 'Yeah, sure.' What was I going to say—no? Either you make $75,000 playing in the NHL or you make $25,000 in the minors. I didn't want to go to the minors."

The good news was that Gilmour learned significant lessons about how to play effectively at both ends of the rink, and he got a lot of experience playing against top lines.

Early on, however, it didn't provide him with a lot of scoring chances. It wasn't until his twelfth game, a 3–2 loss to the Detroit Red Wings, that Gilmour finally scored.

"I had some scoring chances that I missed on, and had

some assists in the first eleven games, but I couldn't buy a goal," he said. "I finally got one on a rebound against Eddie Mio of the Red Wings in a home game.

"There was a shot from the point that hit the goalie. I spun around and got the rebound and just put it five-hole underneath his stick as the goalie was sliding. I was pretty excited, believe me. When the puck goes across the line, you are pretty excited. I know they had me playing a defensive role, but the previous year I had pretty big numbers, so in my own mind I had expectations of scoring. You know in your mind you can score, but you haven't got any goals yet, so when I got that first one, it was a relief."

His first goal did not change his role with the club.

"It didn't matter if we were playing Denis Savard, Wayne Gretzky, or Marcel Dionne, the top centremen in the league at the time, Jacques Demers told me if they go to the bathroom, I am to follow them," Gilmour said with a chuckle. "I pissed a lot of people off. It's not exactly what you want to do, but that was Jacques's game plan, and that's what he wanted me to do. I had to be in their face. If the guy was leaving the zone for a breakout pass, I had to be with him. As time went on, I got more confidence and started to feel I could do more things with the puck. I started to show more creativity. At the same time, my job was to not let the centre I was playing against beat me."

As time went on, however, Gilmour found his confidence and started to chip in more on offence. In fact, he finished the year with 25 goals and 53 points in 80 games.

Gilmour said even though he played on the third line, he was blessed with a couple of nifty linemates in Wayne Babych and Jorgen Pettersson. He laughed when he recalled playing with Pettersson.

"He was a big Swede, and before every game, during warmup, he'd say to me, 'I feel good . . . I'll be high in the slot.'" Gilmour said. "I knew he wasn't going into the corners."

The lessons Gilmour learned about defensive hockey stayed with him over the years, even when he became a scoring sensation.

"You look back on what it did for me and my overall game, I think it prolonged my career," said Gilmour, who won the Frank J. Selke Trophy as the NHL's best defensive forward in 1992–93, a testament to his solid two-way play. "It made me a lot more aware of the defensive side of the game. There's nothing a coach likes better than a guy who is going to play defence as well as offence. The funny thing is, I had 25 goals my first year. I was playing 18 minutes a game. I didn't get to play on the power play, but when there was a good centre on the ice, I was out there checking him, so I got lots of playing time."

In his first year, Gilmour also built a reputation for being a player who wouldn't take any guff. He was small, all right, but he was downright mean, which prompted veteran Brian Sutter to call him Charlie—as in Charles Manson, the convicted mass murderer. That eventually morphed into the nickname "Killer," which stayed with him throughout the rest of his career. There were times throughout his career when Gilmour would go a little over the top in trying to prove his toughness, but early on, Sutter, his roommate for five years, was always there to keep him in check.

"There were guys in the league who were huge, like Behn Wilson and Willie Plett," Gilmour recalled. "I remember Brian telling me, when we would play the Islanders, who had big Clark Gillies, 'You little bugger, don't you dare do anything to wake that guy up. Just let him sleep.' I remember once in Philadelphia, during warmup, there was a guy on the Flyers standing at centre ice, just staring at our team. Finally, I asked Sutter who he was. He goes, 'Don't look at him . . . don't go near him.' Turns out the guy was Randy Holt, a player you really didn't want to mess with."

Holt once had 411 minutes in penalties in one season in the Central Hockey League, and four times he had more than 200 minutes in the NHL. Needless to say, it didn't take much to provoke him, and most opponents tried to steer clear of him, including Gilmour.

Gilmour was traded to Calgary after the 1987–88 season, and he helped the Flames win the Stanley Cup in 1988–89. He scored the Cup-winning goal when he tapped a rebound out of the air, past Patrick Roy in the Canadiens goal. Perhaps his greatest success came with the Toronto Maple Leafs, for whom he served as captain from 1994–95 to 1996–97. At that stage of his career, Gilmour was one of the best and most valuable players in the league. He never won the Hart Trophy as MVP, but he was always in the running.

It was with the Leafs that he scored one of his most memorable goals, when he cut out from behind the net and slipped a backhander past his future teammate Curtis Joseph. He first tried to come out the short side, but teammate Dave Andreychuk and a Blues defenceman were in the way, so he retreated to the back of the net again. Reverting to Plan B, Gilmour took a couple of strides the other way in an attempt to scoot to the other side of the goal, but in an instant, he did a 180 degree spinarama move and, with the path to the front of the net clear, swooped around the goal and crammed a backhander past a startled Joseph in the St. Louis goal, giving Toronto a win in double overtime.

His worst goal ever?

"That came in junior, when we were playing against Belleville," Gilmour said. "There was a delayed penalty, so we had pulled our goalie for an extra forward. I was standing behind their net with the puck. I made a pass to my winger, but he missed it and the puck went all the way down the ice into my team's net. I was thinking, 'Seriously, that doesn't count, does it?' It did."

FOUR

STANDOUT STARS

Previous page: Oft-penalized Tiger Williams was not known for pretty
goals, as he is seen here, crashing into the net of the Vancouver Canucks.
(Graphic Artists/Hockey Hall of Fame)

DAVE "TIGER" WILLIAMS

JANUARY 18, 1975

DAVE WILLIAMS DIDN'T SET OUT to become the most penalized player in NHL history. It just kind of happened. Williams, best known as Tiger because of his perpetual energy and aggressiveness, ran up a whopping 3,966 penalty minutes in fourteen colourful seasons with the Toronto Maple Leafs, Vancouver Canucks, Detroit Red Wings, Los Angeles Kings, and Hartford Whalers.

At first blush, you might think Tiger Williams was little more than a thug who fought his way into the NHL. Nothing could be further from the truth. Unlike a lot of enforcers, Williams could actually play the game. He had skill to go with his ferocity. You don't pop 52 goals and 108 points in 66 games in your third and final year of junior by simply being a fighter.

Even though fighting got him to—and kept him in—the NHL, Williams spent every day of his career trying to be a better player. That said, it was a process in terms of learning exactly what it takes to be a successful pro.

"After three years of junior, where you have been the cock of the walk, you get it knocked out of you pretty quickly in pro," Williams said. "I remember calling my old man and saying, 'What did you guys do to me? You didn't get me prepared for pro.' My dad said, 'How was I supposed to get you prepared? I never had a pair of skates on in my life!' I was so disappointed with the stuff that I didn't know—how to be prepared. I never, from that moment on, came to the rink unprepared. No matter what team I was on, I could run farther than anybody. Being prepared was the one thing you had control of. You don't have control over the guy standing behind the bench who tells you what line you're on and when you go out. But you can control your physical fitness and your mental state of mind."

The thirty-first pick in the 1974 NHL draft, Williams didn't make the NHL on his first crack at it. He played a few exhibition games with Toronto, but was sent to the Oklahoma City Blazers. Williams insists he has no regrets about having to start his pro career in the Central Hockey League.

"The best thing that ever happened to me was being sent to the minors," Williams said. "That was a good thing. When I got called up to Toronto finally, I was leading the team in goal scoring. I learned a lot from those guys down there. We had some guys that were career minor leaguers, and they knew they were never going to play in the apple, which is what they called the NHL. They were great guys, but they knew they were going back to the ranch eventually, or to run their dad's business, and they were living out the final years of their hockey careers. The thing is, you don't want to buy into their philosophy."

Williams didn't allow anybody to stand in the way of his dream of making it to the NHL. If that made him unpopular with his older teammates, so be it.

"I used to go skate by myself in the afternoon, and when the older guys found out, they wanted to hang me," he said. "They said to me, 'If you start doing this crap, we're all going to have to do it.' I said, 'Hey guys, you've gotta do what you've gotta do. I'm not interested in playing my whole career in the minors.'"

Williams fancied himself a tough guy in junior, but he said was shocked when he turned pro.

"Every time I got into a fight that I wasn't looking for, I got the crap kicked out of me," Williams said. "When I played junior, if you got into trouble as a seventeen-year-old, the nineteen-year-olds would look after you. In pro, you come into the league with 300 penalty minutes and they just think you're the guy who is going to fight. The guy who is twenty-five or twenty-six and has played in the minors, they've been around the block. They know when to get you and how to get you."

Williams viewed his time in the minors as a means to an end.

"The whole time I was in the minors, I had the feeling that the Leafs were going to call me the next day," he said. "After every game I played in Oklahoma City, I waited for that call from Toronto. I used to tell the coach, 'Play me wherever you want, but I have to be on the ice all the time.' When I finally got the call, I was very comfortable going up. I had been around the block and I knew what it took to be a successful pro."

Williams may have taken a few lumps along the way, but his hard work and determination didn't go unnoticed. The Leafs were a team in transition, becoming Darryl Sittler's team, and while there was plenty of skill on the club, there wasn't a lot of toughness. Williams knew exactly what his role with the Leafs was when he was recalled from Oklahoma City.

"The year before I arrived in Toronto, the Leafs drafted Lanny McDonald, Bob Neely, and Ian Turnbull in the first round, and then Jack Valiquiette, who scored 68 goals in junior and was their first-round [pick] in 1974, and they never really had what we would call at that time a real, legitimate tough guy," Williams said. "I didn't have to beat anybody out for the role. It's not that I wanted that particular role; it's just the way it happened. You know what it's like—once you get pigeonholed, that's the way people view you. I was simply the man for the job. The guys they had in the minors could fight, but they couldn't play."

Right away, Williams made his mark physically with the Leafs, but it took a while for him to score his first goal.

"It was actually my sixth game, against the Canadiens in Montreal," Williams said. "Ron Ellis passed me the puck as I was skating through the middle into the slot. I got it and fired it as quickly as I could, beating Bunny Larocque on his glove side. Imagine that—I shot the puck and it went in!

"It was a Saturday-night game, and I'll never forget after the game, getting on the pay phone that was outside the dressing room in the old Montreal Forum and calling an old friend, Bernie Jordan, who was a die-hard Montreal fan and who used to let me come over to his house and watch Saturday-night hockey on his colour TV, and I said, 'How do you like your Habs now?'"

Williams had a very productive rookie season with the Leafs for a guy whose main responsibility was to energize the team and defend his teammates. In 42 regular-season games, he managed 10 goals and 29 points with 187 penalty minutes, while in the playoffs he added a goal and 4 points with 25 PIM in 7 games.

When you accumulate 3,966 penalty minutes—more than anyone else in NHL history—people tend to talk about your fighting more than anything else. Williams, however, was a pretty good player, too, scoring 241 goals and 513 points in 962 games. He scored 20 or more goals on four occasions, including a superb 35-goal season in 1980–81 with Vancouver.

The other number that stands out in Williams's career, aside from his penalty total, is 229. That is the number of fighting majors he accumulated during the regular season. They say fighting stops in the playoffs, but that wasn't the case for Tiger. He had 17 fights in 83 post-season games.

Williams was a tough guy right up to the end of his career—and beyond. He recalls an incident in a charity game with complete pride.

"We were playing in Alaska in an oldtimer's game, and Guy Lafleur and Steve Shutt are playing with us," Williams said. "We're playing an Alaskan alumni team, and some of these kids are twenty-four and twenty-five years old. We go out for the first period, and I swear we didn't touch the puck. So in the dressing room, Lafleur is sucking on his eleventh cigarette, and he doesn't normally say a lot, but he looks at me and says, 'The Flower don't lose to no amateurs. You do what you do, and the Flower will do what he does.'

"We go out for the second period, and I tell Shutt, 'If we get the puck, just dump it on their net and get the hell out of the way.' Shutt dumps it in and the goalie grabs it. Well, I ran into the goalie as hard as I could. I knew those kids were coming at me, and when the first guy showed up, I turned around and plowed him. Down he went. The building was full, and the fans started booing. When they stopped booing, we were up 5–3. After the game, we're sitting around having a beer, and Lafleur says, 'Hey Tiger,' and he gives me a thumbs-up.

"The moral of the story is, Lafleur knew how to win. That's why he won five Stanley Cups. He knew how to win, and he knew how to look around a dressing room and decide who has the ability to get us over the hump or change the flow of the game."

Williams, meanwhile, never played on a team that won the Cup. It is something that haunts him to this day. He did have one adventure with the Stanley Cup and fellow enforcer Bob Probert that still makes him laugh.

"When you finish playing and you don't have your name on that Cup, there's a vacuum there—a really big vacuum," Williams said. "We were flying to Afghanistan to visit the Canadian troops, and we had the Cup with us. On the way home, Mike Bolt, who looks after the Cup, is sleeping on the plane. Probie says to me, 'Hey Tiger, have you ever hugged the Stanley Cup?' I said, 'No, we're not allowed to touch it.' Probie says, 'Screw him. He's sleeping.'

"So we open up the box and get the Cup out. I have pictures of Probie and myself lying together with the Cup. Of course, we fall asleep. When Mike woke up, he was furious, but we just laughed. We were like two kids in the candy store."

Williams says he's not the sentimental type, but he still gets a charge from seeing the puck from his first NHL goal. "I was just looking at the puck a few days ago," Williams said. "Nowadays, they give you a plaque with the puck from your first goal, but in my day, if one of your teammates didn't grab the puck out of the net for you, you simply didn't get the puck. You'd have to steal one and pretend that was the puck from your first goal. Mine has a piece of old tape that has turned yellow, but you can still read: FIRST NHL GOAL."

JAROME IGINLA

PROFESSIONAL HOCKEY PLAYERS HAVE a phrase they use, though hopefully not often: "playing guilty." It's when you stay out a little too late the night before a big game and are still feeling the effects of your indiscretion.

Most players are smart enough to know you need to be well rested and in tip-top shape to perform in the NHL, especially early in your career, when you are establishing your reputation, but sometimes circumstances ruin the plan. Take Jarome Iginla, for instance.

Iginla has built a reputation as being one of the most dedicated and prepared professional athletes on the planet, but when it came to making his NHL debut, well, let's just say he was caught off guard.

"I was playing for Kamloops in 1996, and we had lost out in the semifinal of the WHL playoffs, so the guys on the team and I went out," Iginla said. "We were out pretty much all night. It's one of those things all players do at the end of the season. The Flames had told me they were going to bring me up, but I wasn't going to play, so I didn't really take care of myself the way I would if I knew I had a game the next day— especially an afternoon game.

"The next day, the only thing I really had to worry about was getting up and making my flight. I wasn't supposed to be playing, so it was really no big deal. I flew in for the game, and when I got there, I signed my contract that we had agreed to. After I signed, I went down to the dressing room, and the guys were half-dressed, getting ready for the game. I was going around the room, meeting the guys, and finally Ronnie Stern said, 'Okay, kid, enough with meeting the guys. You've gotta get dressed.' I was shocked. The team was almost ready to go out on the ice, and there I was, standing in my street clothes. Some of my teammates in Kamloops told me their billets woke them up and said, 'Jarome's playing with the Flames today.' They couldn't believe it. Neither could I."

The Flames figured they might as well play a hot hand. Iginla had been drafted in the first round, eleventh overall, by the Dallas Stars in the 1995 NHL Entry Draft, but his rights were traded to the Calgary Flames, along with Corey Millen, in exchange for veteran centre Joe Nieuwendyk on December 19, 1995. Merry Christmas!

In three seasons with Kamloops, Iginla scored 102 goals and 236 points in 183 regular-season games and another 26 goals and 56 points in 56 playoff games. In his third year, he established himself both as one of the best players in the league, scoring 63 goals in 63 games and another 16 in 16 playoff games, and a blue-chip pro prospect.

With the Flames trailing 2–0 in their best-of-seven opening-round playoff series against the Chicago Blackhawks, they decided to roll their dice on the kid. That's why he got pressed into service in game three.

"I guess at the end of the day it was good, because I didn't have a chance to get nervous," Iginla said. "I didn't score in that game, even though I had some decent chances. I did get an assist, and I got to play with Theo Fleury and German Titov, two great veterans."

Because he was added to the roster without warning, Susan Schuchard, who raised Iginla as a single mother, and her parents, Rick and Frances, who also played a huge role in raising him, were unable to make it to the game. They were, however, in attendance, along with some of his friends, for game four of the series. And he sent them all home smiling.

"It was pretty cool," Iginla recalled. "I obviously had more time to think about the game and prepare myself to play. I played again with Theo and Titov."

With the score standing at 0–0 in the second period, Iginla scored the first of what would prove to be hundreds of NHL goals.

"I took a pass from Theo, who was positioned at the lower part of the right faceoff circle while I was standing in the slot," Iginla said. "When the puck came to me, I tried to get my shot off as quickly as I could. I aimed low and the puck went under Eddie Belfour's blocker. It was really cool to see that first goal go in. It was something that you had wanted to happen for so long, and yet at the same time it was hard to believe that you actually made the NHL and actually scored a goal in the NHL. It was a great feeling. To score on a great goalie like Eddie Belfour made it extra special."

While the Flames paid a huge price to get Iginla—Nieuwendyk led the Dallas Stars to the Stanley Cup in 1999, one of three he won in his career, and was named most valuable player in the playoffs—Iginla repaid them with some spectacular hockey of his own. One of the most likeable players you would ever meet off the ice, he is a ferocious competitor on the ice—a power forward who will gladly play any style you want, with skill or with brute physical force.

In fact, the year the Flames made it to the Stanley Cup final against the Tampa Bay Lightning, a series the Lightning won in seven games, one of the most memorable moments came when the six-foot-one, 210-pound right winger dropped the gloves to fight fellow superstar Vinny Lecavalier. It was a knock-'em-down, drag-'em-out battle between the best players on both teams that people continue to talk about.

Although he was extremely disappointed at not winning the Cup, the 2003–04 season was still pretty special. Iginla was named captain of the Flames at the start of the year, replacing linemate Craig Conroy, becoming the first black captain of an NHL team. He scored 41 goals that season, tying Ilya Kovalchuk and Rick Nash for the league lead as the three shared the Rocket Richard Trophy. Iginla had also won the prestigious Richard Trophy in 2002, when he led the NHL with 52 goals. He led the 2003–04 playoffs with 13 goals.

Internationally speaking, Iginla helped Canada win the gold medal at the World Junior Championship in 1996, and later two Olympic gold medals, in Salt Lake City in 2002 and in Vancouver in 2010.

Iginla survived his NHL debut and scored in his second game. He said that, after scoring his first NHL goal, he kept a close eye on the clock.

"My goal almost stood up as the game winner, but Chicago tied the game with about ten seconds remaining in regulation time and beat us in triple overtime," he said. "Oh well, it still felt great to get that first one."

BOBBY CLARKE

GIVEN THE FACT THAT Bobby Clarke enjoyed a brilliant Hall of Fame career, it's hard to believe it very nearly didn't get off the ground at all. And what a pity that would have been.

Despite the fact that Clarke was one of the most accomplished junior hockey players in the world, not to mention a seeming blue-chip professional prospect, some potential suitors were scared away because of his diabetes, a condition he was diagnosed with as a teenager. Some teams feared his medical condition would prevent him from handling the daily rigours of playing professional hockey in the best league in the world.

Not Clarke, though. In fact, he seemed quite oblivious to it all. Clarke said he never gave his diabetes a second thought until draft day in 1969, when he was chosen seventeenth overall, despite the fact many teams felt he was, in fact, the best player available.

"I knew players from the Western Hockey League who were taken ahead of me in the draft that I was better than, and it was the first time I ever heard it was because I had diabetes," Clarke said. "I probably lucked out in that, at that time, there was really only one kind of insulin, and your urine test couldn't tell you exactly what your blood sugar really was. I'm quite certain I probably ran a little higher than doctors would have liked, but it also allowed me to have very few low-sugar reactions. There was one at my first Flyers training camp, but it was my fault because I skipped breakfast.

"It was the first time I ever had a reaction in my life, and I had the disease for six or seven years at that point. You eventually pass out because your blood sugar gets so low. I never had another episode after that one."

Clarke said there may have been another reason why he wasn't picked until seventeenth in the draft. The Flin Flon, Manitoba, native, who starred in junior for the hometown Bombers, thinks it had as much to do with geography as anything else. It is laughable now to think that teams actually passed on him after he scored 51 goals in back-to-back seasons with the Bombers, and 168 and 137 points respectively.

"Where I played junior hockey was so far off the beaten path, we hardly got any scouts up there," he said. "Danny Summers, a scout for the Detroit Red Wings, used to come and watch us play a couple of times a year because he was friends with our coach, Pat Ginnell. Otherwise, teams would mostly see us on the road. I never really had any feedback as far as where I stood in terms of being a good junior. I knew I was a good player in the West, but I didn't know how I stood up against other juniors in the two other leagues across Canada."

After using the sixth-overall pick in the draft to select right winger Bob Currier, who never played a game in the NHL, the Flyers rolled the dice with their second choice to take Clarke. This was after the Boston Bruins used the third and fourth picks in the draft to take Don Tannahill and Frank Spring, who played a combined 172 NHL games, and the Toronto Maple Leafs, legendary failures at the draft table, scooped Ernie Moser with the ninth pick. Moser never even made it to the show.

Clarke, meanwhile, got assurance from the Mayo Clinic, at the insistence of Ginnell, that he could indeed play in the NHL if he managed his medical condition.

Once Clarke hit the ice in the NHL, any doubters about his potential and durability were immediately silenced. For the next fifteen years, he became one of the greatest warriors the game has ever known. Even today, decades after his retirement, Bobby Clarke remains the face of the Flyers franchise. Philadelphia has been home to other NHL superstars—the likes of Eric Lindros, Chris Pronger, goaltender Bernie Parent, Dale Hawerchuk, Paul Coffey, and Bill Barber—but none came close to capturing the imagination of the wild Flyers fans the way Clarke, with his flowing, curly locks and two front teeth missing, did in his prime.

Upon his arrival in Philadelphia, Clarke experienced quite a culture shock. Keeping his eye on the puck and his unfolding career, his focus carried him through the day.

"Philadelphia was so huge compared to Flin Flon," Clarke said. "I certainly wasn't used to the traffic. The thing is, I didn't really get too involved with all of that. What I did was simply go to practice and stick closer to the older players. We had a couple of veterans, Billy Sutherland and Wayne Hillman, who were both married and had kids, and they would have me over for dinner. Other than that, I just went to the rink and played hockey. I didn't get involved in the city at all. It wasn't uncomfortable for me."

Like most rookies, Clarke was nervous about his NHL debut, and his first shift in the bigs in 1969 still makes the hair on the back of his neck stand up.

"It was against the Minnesota North Stars, and the first time I got on the ice, the puck hit my stick and Bill Goldsworthy took it away from me and walked in and scored a goal," Clarke said. "I thought, 'Oh man, here I go. I'm done before I start.'"

That, obviously, wasn't the case. He recovered from that faux pas, and his dream of scoring an NHL goal was realized a short while later.

"It was my seventh game, at home against the New York Rangers," Clarke recalled. "Bill Sutherland and I skated in on a two-on-one against their defenceman, Arnie Brown, and their goalie, Ed Giacomin. I got the puck, skating in on the left wing, and I remember putting my head down and slapping it as hard as I could toward the Rangers' net, and it went in.

"It was heaven for a young hockey player. Even though you are only twenty, it is what you have dreamed about your whole life—making the NHL and scoring your first goal. It was a rush. Everybody feels the same about it."

It was absolutely the start of something special. Over the next fifteen years, Clarke scored 358 goals and 852 assists for 1,210 points in 1,144 games and added an additional 42 goals and 77 points for 119 points in 136 playoff games as the Flyers established themselves as the best of the NHL's 1967 expansion teams.

Bobby Clarke was the leader of the Broad Street Bullies, the player others followed into battle. At five-foot-ten and a little under 180 pounds, Clarke did not have the physical attributes that many of his teammates boasted, and yet he was arguably the most feared Flyer of all time—even more than Dave "The Hammer" Schultz, the team's resident goon.

It wasn't long before the Flyers became Clarke's team, and his leadership was rewarded. In 1972–73, his fourth year with the team, he shared the captaincy with veteran defenceman Ed Van Impe. The following season, Clarke was named the team's sole captain, and the Flyers responded by winning back-to-back

Stanley Cups. The captain's C never looked more at home on a player' jersey than on the one Clarke wore for the Flyers.

It was Clarke's burning desire to win and the fact he would do anything—anything!—to achieve victory that made him so dangerous. There is perhaps no greater example of this than the famous 1972 Summit Series, Canada versus the Soviet Union, an eight-game exhibition that would decide hockey supremacy in the world. Canada misjudged its opponent and found itself in a tooth-and-nail battle, but things swung in Canada's favour in game six, when Team Canada assistant coach John Ferguson suggested to Clarke that their team would stand a much greater chance of winning if something could be done to slow down speedy Soviet forward Valeri Kharlamov. Without hesitation, Clarke zeroed in on Kharlamov and broke his ankle with a vicious slash.

The Flyers ruled the NHL through intimidation, and the fearless Clarke was unquestionably their most intimidating force. Under coach Fred Shero, who took over from Vic Stasiuk in 1971–72, the Flyers' philosophy was simple: beat the opposition into submission, knowing the referees can only call so many penalties. It worked. The Flyers would take penalties, but in doing so, scared the daylights out of many of their opponents. With Bernie Parent in net and Clarke leading the penalty killers, they were difficult to score on even when they were shorthanded.

Teams were afraid to play the Flyers, especially in Philadelphia. Jim McKenny, a skilled defenceman with the Toronto Maple Leafs, once said, "When we played at the Philadelphia Spectrum, we would be walking toward the rink, and when we turned around, our team bus was still shaking."

It was amazing the number of players who caught the flu—the Philadelphia flu—when it came time to play the Flyers in their barn. With the likes of Clarke, Schultz, Andre "Moose" Dupont, Don "Big Bird" Saleski, and Bob "Hound Dog" Kelly petrifying opponents, the Flyers led the NHL in points in 1973–74 and 1974–75, their championship years. It wasn't until the Montreal Canadiens matched the Flyers in toughness and exceeded them in skill that Philadelphia's reign of terror came to an end.

Leading this group of tough guys had its challenges, Clarke said. "We had lots of really talented players who, at different times, strayed from playing as good as they should have," Clarke insisted. "I think it was okay because we had enough good players to cover for them. You just had to make sure that guys like the [Rick] MacLeishes and [Reggie] Leaches, guys who drifted, played good when the games were more important . . . and they always did. A guy like Rick MacLeish could have been a Hall of Famer if he had played to the best of his ability on a consistent basis, but he drifted in and out. He would score 50 goals and then drop off a bit. It was just his personality. You just had to make sure in certain games [when] we needed him to play good or we weren't going to win. Those guys could really play hockey, but both of their careers ended early because of their lifestyle."

Clarke, meanwhile, enjoyed a fruitful career, being named the NHL's most valuable player three times. He also won the Bill Masterton Memorial Trophy in 1972 for perseverance, sportsmanship, and dedication to hockey, as well as the Frank J. Selke Trophy as the NHL's best defensive forward in 1983. He was elected to the Hockey Hall of Fame in 1987, and later enjoyed a very successful career in NHL management with the Flyers, Minnesota North Stars, and Florida Panthers.

Today, Clarke is very matter-of-fact about the medical concerns that threatened to sabotage his career.

"I would never allow it to be used as an excuse," Clarke said. "For me, I was a hockey player that had diabetes and not a diabetic hockey player. If I had a bad game, it was just simply because I didn't play well."

It all came down to looking after himself.

"It was no big deal, really," Clarke said years later. "It was just what I had to do to stay alive."

MARK MESSIER

IF YOU WERE TO SCRIPT THE PERFECT scenario for a player scoring his first NHL goal, you'd have to go a long way to beat Mark Messier's story. Imagine playing in your second NHL game in the city you grew up in—Edmonton, Alberta—with your friends and family sitting in the stands.

It gets better.

Imagine, if you will, it is also your mother's birthday. What better present for dear Mom than scoring your first NHL goal! That is exactly how it unfolded for the young man who would develop into perhaps the greatest leader in professional team sports.

At the time, though, Mark Messier was still trying to find his way as a gifted young pro. Moose, as he would become known, was a gritty, ferocious competitor who was fast-tracked to the NHL with a pit stop in the World Hockey Association.

Messier first caught the attention of professional teams when he was a seventeen-year-old playing Tier II junior hockey with the St. Albert Saints, a team coached by his dad, Doug. Doug Messier played professional hockey himself, and he instilled a work ethic into his son that few matched. Doug Messier secured a tryout for Mark with the Indianapolis Racers of the WHA, but Mark was released after just five games. Mark then signed with the Cincinnati Stingers, for whom he scored one goal and 11 points in 47 games.

Messier quickly developed a reputation for paying any price to win. Even though his numbers were low, the hometown Oilers grabbed him with the forty-eighth pick in the 1979 draft, still considered one of the best and deepest drafts ever. Thus, one of the great one-two punches of all time was born—Wayne Gretzky and Mark Messier.

Gretzky was already an established star, having also played the previous season in the WHA. He led the Oilers in scoring as a seventeen-year-old, with 104 points in 72 games in 1978–79, and was the team's marquee player when it joined the NHL the following season. In his first year in the NHL, Gretzky was an instant star, scoring 51 goals and 137 points in 79 games. Messier, meanwhile, took a while to find his offensive stride. He played a more physical game while fine-tuning his other skills.

"Looking back, I only started to excel at the Tier II level just before I went to the WHA," Messier said. "My last year of Tier II, I started to get pretty dominant at that level, when I was seventeen. I was scoring and playing tough. Then I went to the WHA early that year, and I had to develop my offensive skills and game at the pro level, which not too many people did back then and certainly don't do anymore. It seemed to be the right move at the time. I don't have any regrets at all. I was lucky enough to have people around me who were patient in an organization that was starting up. I fell into the right spot."

The Oilers used their first pick in the 1979 draft to choose defenceman Kevin Lowe before picking Messier. With Gretzky, Lowe, and Messier on board, it was the beginning of what would develop into a dynasty, although in Year 1 in the NHL, the Oilers were a middle-of-the-pack team. But that didn't matter to Messier. He was where he had always dreamed of being—playing for the Oilers—and he was determined to take his game to the next level.

"What I did have, more than anything else, was a good understanding of what it means to be a team player," Messier said. "I got that from my dad. I also understood the mental approach to hockey and the intimidation side of things. I wasn't mature and didn't make all the best decisions, but that's what happens when you are eighteen years old and people expect you to be wise beyond your years because you are playing in a win-at-all-costs environment. Very rarely do guys get the opportunity to make mistakes. We were in an environment where we were able to make mistakes on and off the ice, with the understanding that we needed to grow."

The WHA was a rival to the NHL, but in truth, it was small-time compared to the more established league. Messier discovered as much when he played his first NHL game.

"We had played our exhibition games through the smaller arenas of Western Canada, and we weren't thinking the NHL was that big of a step up," Messier said. "The atmosphere in those games really wasn't a lot different from what we were used to. Then we go to Chicago and get our ears pinned back pretty good. We walk up the steps to the ice and we get beer thrown on us. Ten seconds into the game, there's a couple of fights, and the crowd is roaring. That was a tough game."

The Oilers lost that game 4–2, and then headed home for a date with the Detroit Red Wings three nights later. That was when Messier scored his first NHL goal. Messier was nervous about playing in his first home game, but even the fluttering butterflies in his stomach couldn't keep him off the scoreboard on this day.

The Red Wings took a 3–2 lead at 12:53 of the third period on a goal by Dale McCourt, but Messier responded with 2:24 remaining.

"I came down the left wing and got pushed in behind the goal line," Messier recalled. "Just as I got to the net, I reached out with one hand and poked at the puck. It somehow found its way through Rogie Vachon's legs. I couldn't believe it. It really happened so fast. The dream of playing in the NHL, actually being able to wear an NHL sweater and play a game in my hometown in front of my friends and family had really come true. It was a big moment in my life, that's for sure."

It was also a big moment in the history of the Oilers franchise in that Messier's goal guaranteed Edmonton a tie and provided the team with its first-ever NHL point.

There would be plenty of other big moments to rival that one. While Messier would never win a scoring title in the NHL, he did win the Hart Trophy as the league's most valuable player twice and was named winner of the Conn Smythe Trophy as playoff MVP once. Skating alongside Gretzky, he helped the Oilers win four Stanley Cups, and later, after the Great One departed for the bright lights of Los Angeles, Messier led the Oilers to a fifth Cup.

Perhaps his greatest achievement came in the 1993–94 season, when he led the New York Rangers to their first championship in fifty-four years. Trailing the New Jersey Devils 3–2 in the semifinal, Messier boldly guaranteed the Rangers would even the series with a road victory, and then went out and scored three goals in the third period to make his prediction come true. The Rangers wound up beating the Vancouver Canucks in seven games in the Stanley Cup final.

Messier retired as the NHL's second all-time leading scorer behind Gretzky and was inducted into the Hockey

Hall of Fame in 2007. Messier had been the captain of the Oilers, Rangers, and Vancouver Canucks, and the NHL acknowledged Messier's marvellous ability to lead others by creating the Mark Messier Leadership Award in 2007.

Mark Messier navigated his way to the top of the NHL because he arrived with a plan. He wasn't an instant star, but he was dedicated in his attempt to improve. He still marvels at what it takes to be a successful NHLer.

"Even though they have professionalized major junior so it really does mirror the NHL in so many ways with the schedule and travel, I still think there's a huge step moving up to the NHL," he said. "You look at the strength of the players and the speed of the game. I think sometimes we think kids know more than they actually do. More importantly, there is a certain way to act and to be a professional, and that isn't always taught to the kids in junior. At the same time, the player has to show he is willing to change his behaviour to become a professional."

Messier scored 694 goals in 1,756 regular-season games and another 109 in 236 playoff games, but it's his first NHL goal that never escapes his memory.

"I am often asked about scoring goals, and I tell people my most memorable goal was my first because I scored it on my mom's birthday," Messier said.

STEVE YZERMAN

OCTOBER 5, 1983

A STRONG CASE COULD BE MADE that Steve Yzerman is the second most famous player to ever play for the Detroit Red Wings—behind, of course, Mr. Hockey, Gordie Howe. However, when Yzerman burst onto the scene in 1983, he was merely a baby-faced teenager trying to catch on with a team that hadn't made the playoffs for five years. The fourth-overall pick in the 1983 NHL Entry Draft behind Brian Lawton, Sylvain Turgeon, and Pat LaFontaine, Yzerman had established himself as a talented junior hockey scoring ace with the Peterborough Petes, but it remained to be seen whether he could translate that into success at the professional level.

Back then, the NHL was a big man's league, and Yzerman stood barely five-foot-ten and weighed less than 180 pounds. The native of Cranbrook, British Columbia, who was raised in Ottawa, wasted no time establishing himself as a key member of a team that had clearly turned a corner, scoring in his very first NHL game in Winnipeg. It wasn't exactly a defensive gem—the final score was 6–6—but that was the way the Red Wings played in those days. They were all offence, all the time, with little regard for defensive play. And it would stay that way until Bryan Murray took over as coach in 1990. Of course, Scotty Bowman took things to even greater heights when he became the Red Wings' coach in 1993.

When Yzerman joined Detroit in 1983, it was his offence that most appealed to the Red Wings. He recalls his first big-league goal, scored in the season opener against the Winnipeg Jets, as if it was scored yesterday.

"I got the puck near the blue line and stated to drive to the net from the right side," he said. "As I got there, I switched to my backhand and shot. Their goalie, Doug Soetaert, made the save and the rebound came back to me. I couldn't believe how much net I had to shoot at."

Yzerman says he was thrilled that his dad, Ron, was in Winnipeg to watch his NHL debut. It added to the lustre of scoring in his first game.

"It was awesome," Yzerman says. "I remember being elated that I scored, but also being relieved. You look forward to scoring your first NHL goal, and it was amazing to get it in my first game."

Technically, even though it was the start of the regular season, Yzerman was playing with the Red Wings on a tryout basis. Since he was just eighteen years old and still had two years of junior eligibility remaining, there was a possibility he could be returned to Peterborough.

In reality, there was no way Yzerman would be sent back to play junior. The Red Wings were a team lacking an identity, and Yzerman was to become the face of the organization. He made an immediate impact, leading Detroit in goals, with 39; assists, with 48; and, obviously, points, with 87. He was the runner-up for the rookie-of-the-year award, which went to Buffalo Sabres goaltender Tom Barrasso. Detroit had its first hockey superstar in years, a young man who would become the NHL's youngest captain, at twenty-one years old, in 1986; he would wear the C for twenty years, until his retirement. He was a breath of fresh air for an organization that had been spinning its winged wheels and remains the longest-serving captain in NHL history.

It's not that the team lacked quality people. On the contrary, a number of Red Wings players from the 1983–84 club actually went on to successful coaching careers in the NHL, including Ted Nolan, Colin Campbell, and Barry Melrose. Campbell, in fact, became the NHL's senior vice-president. Another member of the '83–84 Red Wings was a little-known goaltender by the name of Ken Holland, who became the Red Wings' general manager—Yzerman's boss—and was the mastermind behind three Stanley Cup–winning teams.

Still, from the day Yzerman first laced up his skates in Detroit, he took over the Red Wings. If Yzerman was being looked upon as a saviour for a floundering Original Six franchise, he didn't feel the pressure.

"There really weren't any expectations on me in terms of supplying the team with offence," Yzerman says. "That said, I was told there were a few spots open, and my play would determine whether or not I would stay or be returned to junior."

Early in his career, Yzerman was an offensive specialist who cared little about his defensive play. That was reflected in his plus-minus rating, a statistic that grew more important as teams began paying closer attention to defensive play. He was minus-17 in each of his first two seasons and minus-24 in Year 3. Ouch! Eventually, he grew to understand the importance of combining his natural flair for scoring with a greater determination to prevent the opposition from scoring when he didn't have the puck. He then blossomed into one of the NHL's most prolific two-way performers, ultimately winning the Frank J. Selke Trophy in 2000 as the NHL's best defensive forward. Talk about a turnabout!

Although he played the majority of his career in an era when Wayne Gretzky and Mario Lemieux dominated statistically as the top two centres in the NHL, Yzerman enjoyed his share of glory, too. Not only did he lead the Red Wings to three Stanley Cup championships—in 1997, 1998 (when he was awarded the Conn Smythe Trophy as most valuable player in the playoffs), and 2002—he was named to the NHL's First All-Star Team in 2000 and played in ten NHL All-Star Games. Yzerman concluded his twenty-three-year career with 692 goals and 1,755 points in 1,514 games. He was honoured with the Lester B. Pearson Award as the NHL's best player as voted by his peers in 1989 and won the Bill Masterton Trophy for perseverance, sportsmanship, and dedication to hockey in 2003.

Yzerman also made a splash on the international hockey stage, helping Canada win the Canada Cup in 1984 and a gold medal at the 2002 Winter Olympics in Salt Lake City. He retired in 2006 as the NHL's sixth all-time leading scorer and was rightfully inducted into the Hockey Hall of Fame in 2009. *The Hockey News* ranked Yzerman the sixth best player in the post-expansion era.

So highly regarded was Yzerman at the time of his retirement that he stepped right into a front office job with the Red Wings, joining the organization's management staff as vice-president and alternate governor. He also served as general manager of Team Canada at the World Championship and was the executive director of Canada's men's Olympic hockey team at the 2010 Winter Olympics in Vancouver.

The pressure for the Canadian men's team to win the gold medal at home was colossal, yet that is exactly what they did. Yzerman pieced together a team that was mostly young—with a sprinkling of valuable veterans—fast, and highly skilled. It took overtime in the gold medal game, but Canada defeated the United States on a goal by superstar Sidney Crosby to claim gold.

Asked about Yzerman's most important goal, many refer to his heroics in double overtime in game seven of the 1996 Western Conference semifinals against the St. Louis Blues. It's hard to argue with that. Yzerman stole the puck from Wayne Gretzky at the Detroit blue line, slithered through the neutral zone, and then unleashed a sixty-foot slapshot that handcuffed Blues goaltender Jon Casey.

But his illustrious career started with that goal in game one in Winnipeg in 1983.

"To be honest, I wasn't really thinking about scoring in that game," Yzerman recalls modestly. "You are kind of in survival mode in your first NHL game. I was just trying to play well enough to earn my next shift. It really was a thrill. When you think back on all the goals you scored, the first one is definitely one that quickly comes to mind."

JEAN BELIVEAU

IT'S HARD TO SAY WHO WAS happier when Jean Beliveau scored his first NHL goal: Beliveau himself, or the Montreal Canadiens organization. Beliveau was an amazing junior hockey star with the Quebec Citadelles, but the Canadiens were having a little trouble getting him to sign on with the organization. The Canadiens viewed him as the future centrepiece for the NHL's most celebrated organization and would go to any length to ensure that he spent his career wearing the *blue, blanc, et rouge*.

It's not that Beliveau didn't want to play for the Canadiens. On the contrary, Beliveau simply resented the fact that, at the age of fifteen, signing a C form would have bound him to play for the Montreal Canadiens from a certain date and for a specific salary, he wasn't ready to make the commitment. He didn't feel he should be subjected to a standard offer when he was clearly better than most players his age.

Beliveau ultimately signed a different contract agreement, a B form, which meant he would play for the Canadiens if he ever decided to turn pro. However, he wasn't locked into a specific salary, which meant he could negotiate for more money. Beliveau was never a confrontational man, yet he knew he was a special player and didn't want to be paid the same as everybody else. In this regard, he was willing to push the envelope a bit.

"The B form meant if I ever played professional hockey, it would only be for the Montreal Canadiens, and that was my dream," Beliveau said. "Teams had negotiation lists, and they were allowed, according to league rules, to put three names on their list. The Canadiens were anxious for me to sign one of those three forms so they could then move me onto their reserve list. They wanted me to get off the negotiating list and on the reserve list so they could put somebody else onto the negotiating list. I didn't want to sign anything until I finally signed the B form a couple of years later."

In the meantime, Beliveau was content to play hockey in Quebec City, where he was a budding superstar, first with the junior Citadelles and later with the senior Aces. The Canadiens, however, wouldn't give up their pursuit and called him up. It was the start of a beautiful relationship, even if there were a few bumps on the road lying ahead.

"I was still a junior," Beliveau recalled. "At that time, we were allowed to play three games with the NHL team."

Beliveau made his NHL debut on December 16, 1950, along with future teammate Bernie Geoffrion, in a 1–1 tie against the Chicago Blackhawks. Geoffrion, who was also a junior-aged star, scored the Habs' only goal, while Beliveau made his mark with nine shots on goal and was the game's first star.

Even though he was not a full-time member of the Canadiens, Beliveau was delighted to finally be skating in the red, white, and blue of his favourite team.

"There's no doubt it was a thrill," Beliveau said years later. "I was nervous, even though I had been invited to their training camp the previous two years. Still, when the game was over, I knew I could be a success in the NHL."

After the game, Beliveau returned to the Citadelles, but six weeks later, with Rocket Richard and Billy Reay under the weather, Beliveau, Geoffrion, Dick Gamble, and Hugh Currie were summoned by Montreal for a game against the slumping Blackhawks, who had dropped nineteen games in a row. This time Beliveau found the back of the net in a 4–2 win for the Canadiens. The goal was scored at 9:32 of the first period and was assisted by Hal Laycoe.

"It was my second game when I scored my first goal against Harry Lumley," Beliveau said. "What I remember most is being told to get to the net as quickly as possible, which I did. The puck found my stick, and I shot it into the goal. It all happened very quickly."

As much as Beliveau enjoyed his time with the Canadiens, he also knew the NHL wasn't his only option. After graduating from junior, twenty-year-old Beliveau remained in Quebec, where he was making more money than he would have by joining the Canadiens—more than NHL stars Gordie Howe and Rocket Richard, in fact. He really had no desire to leave, and yet, he would attend the Canadiens' training camp at the start of each year. Beliveau stayed with the Quebec Aces for two more years, although he did play three games with the Canadiens in 1952–53, during which he scored five goals.

The Canadiens finally won out in October 1953, signing Beliveau to a five-year, $100,000 contract. Unsubstantiated legend has it that the Canadiens purchased the entire Quebec Senior Hockey League and turned it into a professional circuit, forcing the big guy to join the Habs.

Although the money was equal to what he was earning in Quebec, it gave Beliveau the opportunity to make his dream come true. For the next eighteen years, Beliveau was the toast of the town in Montreal, leading the Canadiens to ten Stanley Cups. He was team captain for the final ten years of his career and scored 507 goals and 1,219 points in 1,125 regular-season games. Beliveau added another 79 goals and 176 points in 162 games.

They called him "Le Gros Bill," but his nickname could very well have been Gentleman Jean. Although Beliveau was a big man at six-foot-three and 205 pounds, he was graceful and generally played within the confines of the rules. That didn't mean he was a pushover, though. Twice in his career, Beliveau topped the 100-penalty-minute mark.

The smooth-skating centre was named the NHL's most valuable player twice, in 1955–56 and 1963–64, and won the Conn Smythe Trophy as playoff MVP in 1965. He led the NHL in scoring during the 1955–56 season, when he scored 47 goals and 88 points in 70 games, outdistancing Gordie Howe of the Detroit Red Wings by nine points. He was inducted into the Hockey Hall of Fame in 1972 and was ranked seventh among *The Hockey News*'s top 100 players of all time in 1998.

Upon his retirement, Beliveau remained with the Canadiens organization as an executive and had his name engraved on the Cup another seven times. The iconic Beliveau was offered the position of governor general of Canada in 1984, but turned it down to help his daughter, Helene, raise her two children.

Looking back, it seems funny that Beliverau was ever involved in a conflict with the Canadiens, especially one that was only resolved after the team bought an entire amateur league in Quebec to get him. To have success right out of the gate was a exceptional thrill that he still recalls.

"It was a special situation because there had been so much publicity suggesting I didn't want to join the Montreal Canadiens and how I wanted to stay in Quebec," Beliveau said. "Then, to come up and score a goal in your second game, brought me great joy and satisfaction. I was certainly very happy."

ROD BRIND'AMOUR

APRIL 11, 1989

EVEN THOUGH HE WAS THRILLED beyond belief to suddenly find himself in the NHL at eighteen years of age in 1989, Rod Brind'Amour was keenly aware that his arrival wouldn't necessarily be greeted as good news for some members of the St. Louis Blues.

"We [Michigan State] lost out in the Final Four, and that night, after the game, I signed with the Blues and flew right to St. Louis," Brind'Amour said. "The Blues' regular season had just ended, so I started when the playoffs opened. It was probably the most nerve-racking time of my whole life. Think about the timing of it: you are joining a new team just when their playoffs are starting. They have played the whole year together, and here comes this kid who is going to take someone's spot . . . someone's job. It was tough."

Very perceptive for a teenager. Brind'Amour also knew that if there was one way to win his new teammates over, it was to show them that he could indeed help the hockey team. So that is exactly what he did.

"I was very fortunate that the first game I got into, I scored on my first shot," he said. "Then I was automatically one of them and I was helping them win. It didn't matter that I was taking someone's spot, because I was contributing. The best part about it was I scored on my next shot in the next game I played in. It was two games, two shots, and two goals. That opened the door to me being accepted."

It also opened the door on a successful twenty-one-year career, during which he would captain the Carolina Hurricanes to the Stanley Cup and become recognized as one of the game's best two-way players—a solid contributor on offence, but also a shutdown centre who could make life miserable for the opposition's top forwards. Twice, Brind'Amour was named the NHL's best defensive forward.

"That's the way I always played," he said. "I was never the best player scoring the most goals. I mean, I scored a lot, but I was never *that guy*. I played defence for a couple of years when I was younger. My dad, who was my coach, put me back there, and I hated it, but he said it was the best thing for me, and at the end of the day, I think it was. It taught me that side of the game—defending. Some guys are obviously better goal scorers and playmakers, but I think you have to play both ends of the rink."

Upon his arrival with the Blues, Brind'Amour watched from the press box as his new team faced off against the Minnesota North Stars in the opening round of the Stanley Cup playoffs. It was a great opportunity to observe and learn about the NHL game. When he finally got the call, he felt ready to go.

After an uneventful first period in his NHL debut, Brind'Amour hit pay dirt in the second.

"I only had three shifts in the first period; just enough to get my feet wet and get comfortable playing in a new league," Brind'Amour said. "On my first shift in the second period, there was a faceoff, and the puck went back to the point. Somebody fired a bullet that hit Minnesota's goalie, Jon Casey, and there was a rebound. The puck was just lying there. The other team's centre had let me go, and it was a good bounce that came to me and I just put it into the empty net."

Brind'Amour knew a thing or two about scoring, having just come off a fabulous freshman season with Michigan State University, during which he scored 27 goals and 59 points in 42 games, but he was absolutely stunned to suddenly have his first NHL goal.

"I was shocked," Brind'Amour said. "I was thinking, 'Did this just really happen?' The whole notion of me even being there was a shock, and then being able to score right away in a playoff game. Wow! The North Stars called a timeout after I scored, so there was this long pause during which they made the announcement that it was my first NHL goal. I had some time to sit there and take the whole thing in. I was eighteen years old and didn't really know what was going on."

The Blues won the series three games to one and advanced to the second round for a series with the Chicago Blackhawks, but Brind'Amour once again found himself relegated to the press box as a healthy scratch.

"That was kind of surprising after I had scored in my first game," he said. "I figured I'd be right back in there."

The Blues lost the opening game of the series, and then turned to Brind'Amour to come in and help them get back on even turf.

"Not only was I back in the lineup, I actually got to start the game at centre," Brind'Amour said. "It was a great feeling, and I scored nine seconds into the game. It was a slapshot off the wing that went between the goalie's legs. I won the faceoff back to our defenceman, and he flipped the puck toward the Blackhawks' zone. Their defenceman moved up on it and it went over his head. I went by him and just drilled a slapshot that went in. Two shots; two goals. I thought it was too easy."

Brind'Amour wound up playing in three more games in that series, which the Blackhawks won in five games. When the next season rolled around, there was no trepidation about returning to the Blues. Even though he had just turned nineteen, Brind'Amour had proven himself and was just one of the boys. He wound up fifth in team scoring with 26 goals and 61 points in 79 games.

There was one thing, however, that set Brind'Amour apart from most of his teammates—and from most players in the NHL, for that matter. Long before others started lifting weights to increase their size and strength, Brind'Amour was pumping iron in an effort to make himself stronger. Actually, he started off pumping *plastic*.

"I was about twelve, and my dad was coaching me," Brind'Amour recalls. "He bought me some plastic weights and told me I had to do something different than the other kids were doing if I wanted to get better. Nobody back then was doing that kind of thing, so every morning, I'd go down to the basement and do a little weight-training routine, and then, in the afternoon when I got home from school, I'd do it again. I'd do fifteen to twenty minutes in the morning and fifteen to twenty minutes after school. A couple of years of that, and I noticed I was getting a little bigger. Obviously, I took it to the next level when I got older, but getting that little jump on my physical training when I was young seemed to give me an edge over a lot of kids."

Brind'Amour, who would become known as "Rod the Bod" in his NHL playing days, just couldn't get enough of the weight room. When he was in college at Michigan State, he'd even work out in the gym after games. In fact, he credits his decision to play college hockey rather than major junior as one of the reasons why he was able to accelerate his arrival in the NHL.

"College was great for me," Brind'Amour said. "Even though I was only there for a year, the atmosphere was amazing. They would play Friday and Saturday nights, and then you basically had the whole week to train and work on your game. I still think that is the great thing about the college game compared to playing junior. In junior, you can't really work on your body. You have so many games, and you don't really have time to get physically mature. The great junior kids come out and can obviously play, but there are a lot of guys who would have benefited if they had more time to work on their bodies and work on their skills."

The highlight of any professional hockey player's career, naturally, is winning the Stanley Cup. Brind'Amour not only got to experience that, he was the one, as captain of the Hurricanes, who accepted the championship trophy from commissioner Gary Bettman. In fact, there were some who thought he tore the Cup out of Bettman's hands during the presentation. What most people don't know, however, was what *almost* happened.

"It is funny. We had just come back from the lockout the year we won the Cup, so there was a lot of resentment by the players toward Bettman," Brind'Amour said. "You think it's all his fault that we had no hockey for a year, and the players were still pissed at him. We used to talk amongst ourselves, and we decided if we won the Cup, we were going to pick him up, carry him over to the penalty box, and drop him in it. We were going to make a scene.

"People give me a hard time because they think I just grabbed the Cup away from him. The thing is, it was so loud that I couldn't hear a thing he was saying. I just thought it was time to take the Cup and I took it. I really didn't mean any disrespect. At the end of the day, I'm glad we didn't follow through on our plan to drop him into the penalty box."

Brind'Amour is proud of his long and successful career, and still gets a chill thinking about scoring on his first two shots. He couldn't have gotten his NHL career off to a better start. Or could he?

"What no one remembers is in my third game, in Chicago, I actually scored on my next shot—and this was before [the league reviewed goals using] instant replay," Brind'Amour said. "They didn't see the puck go in, so it was waved off. I fired the puck in under the crossbar and it came out quickly. It was clear as day that it went in, but they didn't count it. I could have been three-for-three."

BRENDAN SHANAHAN

NOVEMBER 10, 1987

LONG BEFORE BRENDAN SHANAHAN initiated significant changes in the way NHL hockey is played, helping to save a sport that was suffocating itself, he knew he had to make changes in his own game if he was going to enjoy a prosperous professional career.

It's not as though Shanahan had any grandiose plans of joining the NHL and instantly challenging Wayne Gretzky for the scoring title, but when he went goalless in his first fourteen games, he was more than a little concerned.

"It's funny; I was never called a prolific scorer in junior," Shanahan said. "The most goals I ever scored in my hockey career was 39, in my second year of junior. I thought that was amazing. I don't think I ever scored 39 goals in bantam or midget or peewee. When people would ask me what kind of a hockey player I was, I'd think to myself, 'I don't know. I'm just a hockey player. That's it.' If I needed to score, I'd try to score. If I needed to pass, I'd pass. If someone tried to push our team around, I'd push back."

Being the second-overall pick in the 1987 NHL Entry Draft, Shanahan admits he felt a little pressure to make a good first impression. And while he demonstrated the physical element of his game that would become his trademark in what was to be a glorious twenty-one-year-career, getting that first

NHL goal proved to be a bigger challenge than even he had imagined. Considering Shanahan would ultimately score 656 goals in 1,524 games over those twenty-one years, plus the fact he was coming off a year in which he scored 39 goals in 56 games for the London Knights of the Ontario Hockey League, being held off the score sheet in his first fourteen games was as shocking as it was disappointing. Which perhaps made it all the more thrilling when he did score.

"What's amazing about my first goal is it wasn't one of my typical goals," Shanahan said. "In junior, I was used to having all kinds of time with the puck. I had really good accuracy and could take my time and pick a corner to beat the goalie—in junior. In the NHL, my shots were getting blocked or I just wasn't getting them off. My reaction time was too slow. I also always thought, 'I can get closer.' In junior, you can always beat one more guy.

"My first goal actually opened my eyes. I didn't know I had this kind of a release in me. It was a very standard three-on-two rush—a slow-developing three-on-two—and my centre, Claude Loiselle, crossed in front of me at the blue line and dropped me the puck. We didn't have a lot of speed, and it wasn't a dangerous-looking play, but he dropped the puck to me, and as he did, the New York Rangers defenceman was stepping up on me. I had no time to do anything other than a catch-and-release. I was only doing it because somebody was going to hit me. All of a sudden, the puck popped off my stick and beat John Vanbiesbrouck on a clean shot from just inside the blue line. I was like, 'Whoa! I didn't know I could do that!'

"As much as that shot was a shot that I would hone later in my career, it was just an instinctive move at the time. As I moved along in the NHL, my philosophy became 'quick release.' My first goal was off a quick release, but purely by accident. Later in my career, I would have taken that exact same shot, even if someone wasn't stepping up on me. I just learned that's how you score—by shooting the puck before the goalie is set."

Suddenly, the weight of the world was off his shoulders. In an instant, he had justified the Devils' faith in him.

"It was surreal, but even more significant to me because it was a month into the season," he said. "It wasn't, like, game two. It was game fifteen. I was getting pretty frustrated. I looked up to the heavens. I spun around and didn't know who to look at or where to go. I kissed Claude Loiselle on the cheek. I was on cloud nine. My teammates were all happy for me. It was amazing—a great feeling."

What made the goal even more special was the fact it was the game-winner. The Devils beat the Rangers 3–2 that night, and Shanahan had himself a pivotal deciding goal. Turns out, it was the start of a pattern in his career.

"It was huge to get a game-winning goal against a bitter rival," Shanahan said. "It seemed every time I had a big goal or a milestone goal, it was a game-winner against a rival."

When the season concluded, Shanahan was disappointed with his lack of production. He'd managed just 7 goals and 26 points in 65 games.

"Offensively, I was really disappointed in my first year," he said. "I just felt like I couldn't contribute much. I was a bit of a Marmaduke. My shot wasn't strong. I wasn't strong enough by the NHL standard. I had the will, but I didn't have the body or maturity to play the game at the NHL level. I was a teenage boy. You can be a strong guy for an eighteen-year-old, but you don't know when you come into the NHL that there are hundreds of Dave Babych types who, when you hit them, it's like running into a brick wall. You hear about the guys like Cam Neely and Wendel Clark, but you don't realize that everybody else has man forearms and a man back—grown-up bodies. It takes a while to adjust to playing against men."

That would change over time. As Shanahan matured, he developed into a rugged and dependable two-way performer. He played for five different organizations in his career—the Devils, St. Louis Blues, Hartford Whalers, and Detroit Red Wings—winning three Stanley Cups with Detroit. At six-foot-three and 225 pounds, Shanahan was a tough physical customer who could play the game any way the opposition chose. With 1,354 points in 1,524 games, he could score with the best of them. And with 2,489 career penalty minutes, he didn't mind getting his nose dirty on occasion.

"You know, I think that I always had confidence in my ability to compete, no matter who that was against," Shanahan said. "I wasn't thinking, 'I'm going to go to the NHL and score at will.' I always had a confidence that I could beat better players or beat strong players, and that's probably the result of growing up the youngest of four boys. I usually had a mountain to climb. I usually went into most things as an underdog."

As great a player as Shanahan was, he may have made his most significant contribution to the game off the ice. During the lockout in 2004–05, Shanahan gathered some of the biggest names in hockey, from all different facets of the sport, to talk about ways to make the game more interesting. Sadly, hockey had become bogged down with defensive-minded coaches who encouraged their players to hold and obstruct the game's most creative players. Third- and fourth-line players often had more to do with the outcome of games than the superstars who made the most money and skated on the top lines. Hockey had become boring.

"I actually thought I was just finally organizing something that the players had been complaining about for years and years," Shanahan said. "What motivated me to do it in that particular year, during the lockout, was seeing some of the interviews of the Hall of Fame class that year. That was the year three great defenceman—Ray Bourque, Paul Coffey, and Larry Murphy—went into the Hall. They were talking about the game and how it had sort of gotten away and just wasn't the game they had grown up playing. They made all these great points, and the next day in the newspaper there was nothing. I thought, 'How can these guys make all these great statements and I sit around on the bus and plane with all these players who have great ideas on how to improve the game, yet no one ever organizes these ideas?' That was my motivation: to give all the stakeholders a voice. The ideas coming out of Toronto weren't my ideas; I simply organized the meeting and gave a platform for all the stakeholders to speak.

"There were no lead changes, and third- and fourth-liners could neutralize the stars. Better players than me had talked about the problems in the game, and I think what helped me do this was that I wasn't a super-talented player whining. The old style actually benefited me. The rule changes probably shortened my career by a year or two. I wasn't some soft finesse player looking for an edge.

"I'm not a fence-sitter. I'm definitely a side-taker. I don't profess to be smarter than anybody else. I actually love to surround myself with people who think differently than me. What I try to do as much as possible is break down walls that prevent communication. I thought it was crazy that coaches, referees, managers, and players didn't get in the same room to share their perspectives before we came up with rule changes. You'd have an idea, and it sounds great, and then you'd get in a game and the refs would say, 'This doesn't work.' It was like, 'Well, it's too late now; it's a rule.' You'd change something about the goalies, and then the goalies would say, 'That's not going to work. Why do you make a change about goaltending or the crease without asking the goalies?' To me, what was broken was the model for how we make decisions."

What become known as the Shanahan Summit had a distinct and positive outcome in terms of the game becoming more wide open, with an emphasis on speed and skill. Young stars like Sidney Crosby and Alexander Ovechkin were suddenly able to show their skill without impediment.

Upon retiring as a player, Shanahan joined the NHL front office as the vice-president of hockey and business development. He continues to look for ways to make the game better.

"I think back to some of my high school friends, and I wonder what they think of my career," Shanahan said. "I played high school hockey for Michael Power in Toronto, and I was just this big, goofy tenth-grader that was playing on the senior hockey team. I wasn't real smart, but I was enthusiastic. I'm sure my old teammates must scratch their heads and laugh that I have had this career and I have been able to have a life in the NHL. What I feel is a real gratitude that I grew up loving the game of hockey like any other kid, and I am now in a position and have a job where I can do my best to help and influence the game."

MARTIN ST. LOUIS

BY 2000, MARTIN ST. LOUIS knew he had reached a crossroads in his career. After years of banging his head against the wall, trying desperately to get the recognition he felt he had earned, St. Louis decided to take matters into his own hands. Nineteen games into his fourth professional season, and once again finding himself in and out of the lineup of the expansion Tampa Bay Lightning, St. Louis knew it was time to put up or shut up.

"I scored my first goal of the season about twenty games in—a shorthanded goal," St. Louis said. "Even though I got that goal, I felt my days in the NHL were numbered, and I needed to do something. If I couldn't play on the Tampa Bay Lightning at that time, where was I going to play?

"I figured I was going to go down swinging. If this was going to be my last few games in the NHL, I was going to show people what I could do. If it works, great. If it doesn't, what have I lost? Instead of trying to play safe, I tried to picture myself playing in college and picture myself playing in the American league. I visualized how I did things my whole life before I got to the NHL and changed my game. I started playing the way I had my whole life, and I started playing well. The better I played, the more they played me."

After a successful college career at the University of Vermont, St. Louis spent the first three years of his pro career bouncing between the minors and the NHL with the Calgary Flames. Some players who had been scoring stars in college might have been put off by being played mostly on the fourth line in the NHL, but St. Louis said he understood the process.

"I didn't feel like I was getting cheated when they played me on the fourth line," he said. "I just wasn't doing anything to separate myself from anybody else. Why should I be in the lineup, just because I could skate? Was I really showing my speed? I wasn't a first-round pick. I wasn't somebody they had invested a lot of money in so they were going to give me the benefit of the doubt. If that is the case, you have to do something to separate yourself from six or seven guys in the team who are in the same boat.

"I started to do things to separate myself from the other guys in the group. What could I do differently to help this team win more? I started producing, and they played me more. In my second 20 games, I got 15 points. I was up to the third line, but if we had injuries I would be moved up to the second line or the top line. I also started getting some power-play time. I scored 18 goals that year, which is pretty good, considering I didn't score my first goal until the twentieth game."

Martin St. Louis, one of the smallest players in the NHL, had arrived. In fact, once he found his comfort level, he excelled, helping the Lightning win the Stanley Cup in 2003–04, the same year he led the NHL in scoring and was named the Hart Trophy winner as the league's most valuable player.

Although the NHL's *Official Guide and Record Book* lists him as standing five-foot-nine, that is a little generous. He's probably closer to five-foot-seven, but stocky and rock solid. Size came into play when it came to choosing between playing college hockey in the United States or major junior hockey.

"The year before the midget draft, I was playing midget AAA and I was leading the league in scoring," St. Louis said. "Around Christmastime, there was a big midget tournament—Quebec against all the other provinces—and I didn't get picked to be on that team. I was the leading scorer of the league where they took most of the players from. I was disappointed and didn't quite understand it. Those were signs that really pushed me toward the college route. You're talking the early nineties, and getting drafted to the NHL as a small guy was very, very difficult. There weren't many guys my size playing in the league. Guys like Theo Fleury and Cliff Ronning gave me hope, but it became clear to me, most likely it would be hard to make it.

"Colleges really wanted me, where with junior, it was like they were going to do me a favour. I got recruited by many schools. I felt wanted, and at the same time, I got an education out of it. After my freshman year, the junior teams came knocking on the door. I had no interest then."

In his second season at Vermont, St. Louis was named the ECAC player of the year. The following year, his junior season, St. Louis scored 29 goals and 85 points in 35 games, giving him 67 goals and 207 points in 103 games. Suddenly, he was a hot ticket, and NHL teams came calling, offering as much as $150,000 simply to sign an NHL contract. While St. Louis may not have any regrets about how his career has played out, in hindsight, not signing may have been a mistake.

"I figured after taxes and after I bought a car, there wouldn't be much left," he said. "I was one year away from graduating, and I figured if the offers were there now, they'd be there for me a year from then."

Sounds good in theory, but it didn't turn out that way. St. Louis had a decent fourth year at Vermont, but his numbers slipped a bit. At the end of the year, no NHL teams expressed interest in signing him. There was a tryout with the Ottawa Senators, but it didn't really amount to much.

St. Louis wound up signing a two-year deal (with an escape clause if an NHL team wanted to sign him) with Cleveland of the International Hockey League. He scored 16 goals and 50 points in 56 games, played in the IHL all-star game, and caught the eye of the Calgary Flames, who signed him to a contract. He finished the season playing with the Saint John Flames of the American Hockey League.

"Even though I was making the same money playing for Saint John that I did playing for Cleveland—$75,000 a year—I actually took a pay cut by signing with the Flames because I was now getting paid in Canadian dollars, where I had been getting paid in American money with Cleveland," he said with a laugh. "At least I had hope, and hope is a strong magnet. You are drawn to hope, and hope keeps you going. You know you are one phone call away from realizing your dream. When I first went to Saint John, I played the last twenty-five games of the regular season, and then we went all the way to the Calder Cup final. When I first got there, I was on fire, and I felt like the phone was going to ring at any time. It really feeds your fire. I never got the call, but I was happy that I had a good playoff, and the next season I made the Calgary Flames out of training camp. So, one year after not getting a sniff with Ottawa, I am playing in the NHL."

St. Louis started the year playing on a line with stars Theo Fleury and Andrew Cassels, but very quickly slipped down to the fourth line, and then found himself being made a healthy scratch time and time again.

"All my life, I was told I wasn't supposed to make it," he said, "and I think I sold myself short. I second-guessed my abilities a bit. Did I have the ability to play with those guys? Absolutely, but I wasn't ready mentally."

He did, however, manage to score his first NHL goal in his fifth big league game.

"At that point, I had been demoted to the third and fourth lines and I was just trying to stay in the lineup," St. Louis said. "In a game against the Stars in Dallas, there was a big pileup in front of the net, and I came in and just got my stick on the puck. It went up in the air and over the goalie's shoulder. It was kind of a fluke goal. I remember being in a pile of players, thinking, 'Did I score? Did I score?' It was one of those goals where it wasn't clear who got it, but I felt I was the last guy to touch the puck."

By no means did St. Louis have it made now that he had scored in the NHL.

"I had been up and down, and finished the year in the minors," he said. "I only played 53 games with Saint John, but I still led the team in scoring, with 62 points. The following year, I went to camp with Calgary, and they gave me one exhibition game and then sent me down. At that point in time, it was the toughest thing to understand. Here I am, having led their minor-league team in scoring, and I was voted team MVP by the players I played with, and those guys were still at the NHL camp. I had a tough time grasping that. I felt cheated. That was the most discouraged I felt in my career. I had taken so many strides in my career, and I didn't feel like they were giving me a chance.

"Expansion was coming the next season, with Columbus and Minnesota joining the NHL, so I felt there was a little light at the end of the tunnel. There were going to be forty to forty-five new jobs, and I figured I'd have to be one of those guys with the year I had in the American league. I remember telling the Flames' assistant GM, Nick Polano, I was going to go down and lead the AHL in scoring and hook up with one of the new teams; that's how upset I was."

St. Louis scored 15 goals and had 27 points in his first 17 games with Saint John and was recalled by the NHL Flames. It was the last time he'd play in the minors.

"When I got called up, I didn't play an offensive role with the team," he said. "I played a true third-line role, killing penalties and playing against the other team's top lines. For me, it was like a five-month crash course on developing my defensive game. My whole life, I had been an offensive player, and suddenly I was in the role of trying to be smart without the puck. I think those fifty-six games helped me develop into a complete player.

"At the end of the year, I was assured by management they were thrilled by my development. I had a one-year option, and they told me they were going to pick it up. I felt I was back in the process of maturing and developing as a player, but in the next two days, everybody in the front office got fired and there was nobody left pulling for me. The GM was gone, the coach was gone . . . everybody was gone. They had a bunch of high draft picks playing in the minors, and when new management took over, they figured they needed those guys playing in the NHL. I was one of the guys that was going to be cleared out to make room for the others."

Back to the drawing board.

To be exposed in the expansion draft, a player must be under contract to an NHL team. The Flames picked up the option on St. Louis's contract, but when he was not claimed in the draft, they elected to buy him out. St. Louis looks back on the situation and laughs.

"I never got a signing bonus, but now I was being paid by an NHL team to not play with them," he said.

He was now a free agent, and although he had a few teams interested in him, he chose Tampa Bay because he felt his chances of getting playing time with the Lightning was best. He was right, although it took that magical moment when he decided to get back to playing the way he had in college and in the minors before his NHL career really kicked into gear.

When he was named the NHL's most valuable player, it was a time for reflection on where he was versus where he had come from. The kid who was thought to be too small to play major junior hockey was acknowledged as one of the best players in the world.

"Did I come in the back door?" he asked. "Yeah, I did. Did I expect to be on top like that? Heck no. I'd be the first guy to say I even surprised myself. I wasn't surprised that I could play like that, but I was surprised when it all came together for me. I didn't do this on my own; I needed a lot of luck. I played with a lot of confidence that year. I just kept telling myself, 'Why not? Why can't it be me?' Is it weird to be on top of the scoring list? Sure it is. I had to convince myself that's the way it was supposed to be. If you don't feel you deserve it, you'll slip back. In a cocky way, you have to feel that you deserve it."

FIVE

KEEPING IT IN THE FAMILY

Previous page: Gordie Howe with his sons, Mark and Marty. The three would eventually play together for the WHA's Houston Aeros. (Courtesy of the Howe Family)

THE HOWES

OCTOBER 16, 1946 (GORDIE)
NOVEMEBER 19, 1979 (MARK)
DECEMBER 2, 1982 (MARTY)

A LOT OF PROFESSIONAL HOCKEY PLAYERS will tell you that one of the great benefits of their job is being able to bring their kids to the rink. You see it all the time—the sons and daughters of NHL players whipping around the ice before practice. Talk about living the dream! Gordie Howe was certainly no exception, only Mr. Hockey took it a step further.

Not only did Howe bring his kids to the rink, but two years after he retired from the NHL as the highest scorer in league history, he made a stunning comeback to play professionally with his sons, Marty and Mark. To date, the Howes are the only father and sons ever to play together in both the World Hockey Association and the National Hockey League.

There have been a lot of great hockey families over the years—the Patricks, Hulls, Espositos, Sutters, and Staals—but none compare to the Howes. And it was Gordie, a kind and gentle man off the ice, but a warrior who played an eye-for-an-eye, tooth-for-a-tooth game when the puck was dropped, who blazed the trail for what would become one of the most remarkable stories in sports history.

So when the boys were ready to turn pro, Gordie returned to action at age forty-five, joining Marty and Mark with the

Houston Aeros of the World Hockey Association. Gordie had scored 23 goals and 52 points in 63 games in 1970–71, his final season in the NHL, but people wondered how the time off would affect his game.

Howe looked as though he'd never been off skates, compiling 31 goals and 100 points in the WHA en route to being named that league's most valuable player. The WHA was an inferior league to the NHL, but Howe was nevertheless a star.

Who would have guessed that the shy youngster from Floral, Saskatchewan, who showed up to the Red Wings' training camp in 1946, would emerge as one of the greatest players in NHL history, a legend? Howe had attended a tryout with the New York Rangers in 1943, but felt homesick and overmatched and returned home. A year later, he tried out with the Red Wings; they liked what they saw, but at sixteen, he was not quite ready for prime time. So he could get some seasoning, they assigned him to their Junior A affiliate in Galt, Ontario, followed by a year in the minors with the Omaha Knights.

As an eighteen-year-old, he made his mark instantly with Detroit, scoring in his first NHL game. By then, he was a strapping six-footer weighing in at around two hundred pounds, which was pretty big by hockey standards in those days.

Playing on a line with future Hall of Famer Sid Abel and Adam Brown, Howe was feeling right at home in his NHL debut, a home game against the Toronto Maple Leafs on October 16, 1946. As games go, it was an otherwise forgettable evening, a 3–3 draw, but Howe did manage to score his first NHL goal.

Skating in alone on Toronto's Turk Broda, Howe took a shot that was turned aside by the Maple Leafs' goaltender.

"The puck was just lying there, and Ted Lindsay skated past it," Howe said. "He tried to get it, but missed it. I got two whacks at it, and the second one went in. The thing I remember most is the biggest cheer ever went up from the crowd. It was so loud I could barely hear myself think. After the game, Turk congratulated me. I even had him sign the puck. I said to him, 'I'm not trying to be funny, but I had the honour of scoring my first goal against you.' He signed it and gave it back to me."

Nowadays, teams generally get the puck from a player's first goal and put it in a frame along with a copy of the game sheet. Back then, though, players picked up the puck and took it home as a keepsake. Howe cherished the puck from his first goal. He carried it with him wherever he went.

"That puck probably has been in more churches than priests themselves," Howe said when he was eighty-two years old. "It was my good luck charm, and I carried it with me everywhere. I almost lost it one night in Toronto. Somebody went into our dressing room and took it from my dressing stall. I thought it was gone forever, but the guy brought it back. Turns out he just wanted to show somebody the puck from Gordie Howe's first NHL goal."

Howe said he still has that puck, and when he looks at it, it brings back fond memories.

"I had dreamt about scoring my first NHL goal and had worked very hard to get to the NHL," Howe said. "Whenever I was having trouble scoring goals, I would touch the puck, and my luck would change for the better. I put a lot of dents in the backyards of a lot of houses growing up, dreaming about making it to the NHL. I shots pucks at everything and anything I thought was a target."

He must have developed a good eye, because Howe would go on to become the highest scorer in NHL history, leading the Red Wings to four Stanley Cup championships while winning six league scoring titles and six most valuable player awards. After twenty-five years in the NHL with the Detroit Red Wings—more seasons than any other player in league history—Gordie Howe finally retired. That, in itself, is an unprecedented accomplishment. But it wasn't enough for Howe, who longed to play with his sons, who by then were established junior hockey stars playing for the Toronto Marlboros in the Ontario Hockey Association.

When he retired the first time, Howe joined the Red Wings' front office staff. However, he wasn't satisfied with his duties, which really came down to being a spokesman for the team. In 1973, his wife, Colleen, who would become the family's agent and business manager, negotiated a deal with Houston of the WHA that would enable Gordie, Marty, and Mark to play on the same team. The Howes would play together for seven years in the WHA, and when that league folded, the trio, at that stage playing for the New England Whalers, stayed together as the organization was one of four that were brought into the NHL. Playing with his sons was a dream come true, but playing with them in the NHL, well, that just made it so much sweeter.

At the age of fifty-one, Howe returned to the league he once ruled. His sons, who grew up hanging around the Detroit Red Wings locker room, were by his side. At least they were for training camp. While Gordie and Mark made the team—a club that included legends Bobby Hull and Dave Keon— twenty-five-year-old Marty was assigned to Springfield of the American league.

That gave twenty-four-year-old Mark the opportunity to beat his older brother to the punch in terms of scoring his first NHL goal. The funny thing is that, unlike most NHLers, Mark didn't think getting the goal—which came on November 19, 1979, at 1:31 of the opening period of a 6–3 win over the Los Angeles Kings—was such a big deal.

"I just remembered crossing over the blue line and I fired a thirty-five-to-forty-foot wrist shot that snuck into the corner of the net," Mark said. "The biggest thing about the goal was their goalie, Ronnie Grahame, and I were teammates in Houston, and he was one of the ushers in my wedding. It wasn't much of a goal, really. Just a shot that went in.

"For me, I didn't even really look at it as my first goal. I know a lot of sports writers say that's my first goal, but if I had been in the NHL six years earlier, I would have had it back then. I had over two hundred goals in the WHA. To me those were important goals, too."

Mark said his first WHA goal, scored in Vancouver against Pete Donnelly, who was from the Detroit area, is the goal he remembers most fondly.

"To me, that was far more important," he said. "It was my first goal as a professional hockey player."

In fact, Mark didn't think it was such a big deal to finally be playing in the NHL, though he said it was a thrill to play with his father.

"I played on his line for six years, until they moved me back to defence," Mark said. "The best part about it was realizing what a great player he was. The thing I really appreciated in the first two years is that he came out of retirement and we played in Houston and he won the MVP one year and probably should have won it the other year. He was forty-three, forty-four years old and you get a true appreciation of just how good he really is when you play with him every day.

"I went to nearly every game he played in Detroit with the Red Wings, but you get a much truer sense when you see him in practice every day and you see all the little things he does well that you just can't see from the stands."

Mark Howe had a very distinguished NHL career, scoring 197 goals and 742 points in 929 games. Marty had a rough first year in the NHL. Aside from starting the year in the minors, he suffered a broken arm that kept him on the sidelines for half the year. The Whalers called him up late in the season, and he stayed with the team through the playoffs. He didn't score in the six regular-season games he dressed for, but Marty counted his first NHL goal in the playoffs . . . with a little help from Dad.

"It was against Montreal, and I think Gordie actually bounced the puck back to me at the point," Marty recalled. "I slid toward the middle of the blue line while he went to the front of the net. I don't know how he did it—the defenceman must have pushed him or something—but somehow Gordie just ran into the goalie. Basically, all I had to do was hit the open net. When I saw what was happening, I just put it up in the air and it went right into the middle of the net."

Hmm, is there any chance Gordie might have taken the goalie out accidentally on purpose?

"You know, I would say so," Marty said with a guilty laugh. "He had an excuse because the defenceman ran into him, and I believe he took advantage of the opportunity that was presented to him and wiped out the Canadiens' goalie. The goalie was fair game at that point. It was different rules back then."

Not that he is the vindictive type or anything, but scoring against the Canadiens was even sweeter since it was Montreal that had originally drafted Marty, fifty-first overall, in 1974.

Like his younger brother, Marty didn't think there was anything particularly special about being a Howe and playing in the NHL.

"You go into the locker room and put the jersey on, and I don't care what league you're playing in, it was a game that you played with your teammates," he said. "I didn't put any significance on being a member of the Howe family while playing in the NHL."

Maybe he didn't, but the rest of the world certainly did.

THE STAALS

OCTOBER 23, 2003 (ERIC)
OCTOBER 12, 2006 (JORDAN)
NOVEMBER 14, 2007 (MARC)

HENRY AND LINDA STAAL didn't exactly think they would be starting a family farm team for the National Hockey League when
they built their backyard rink. It just turned out that way.

The Staals, who live in Thunder Bay, Ontario, constructed
a 100-by-50-foot rink in the backyard on their sod farm, and
their four sons, Eric, Marc, Jordan, and Jared, honed their
impressive skills in competitive family games. With all that
space and two-on-two games—generally Eric, the oldest,
born in 1984, and Jared, six years younger, pitted against the
two middle brothers, Marc and Jordan, born in 1987 and
1988, respectively—the boys quickly developed into ultra-
competitive and highly skilled players.

The Staal boys all range between six-foot-three and six-
foot-four and between 200 and 215 pounds. Eric, Jordan, and
Jared all play forward, while Marc is the lone defenceman
among the group. Eric is the most supremely offensive talented, while Jordan quickly established himself a gifted two-
way player when he debuted in the NHL at just eighteen years
of age. Marc generally takes care of business in his team's zone,
but has an offensive upside, too. Jared, a checking forward, is
working his way toward the NHL through the minors.

The Staals' homemade rink was quite a setup to behold. It had regulation-size boards—mostly gathered from the local rink when its boards were replaced—proper nets, and an elaborate lighting system that allowed the boys to continue playing deep into the evening. For the Staal boys, hockey was all that mattered. They ate, drank, and slept the game. The boys would hit the rink first thing in the morning, and it was all Henry and Linda could do to get them to come into the house in the evening.

The parents would call the boys in at night, and sometimes their pleas were ignored. They would turn off the rink's lights; after a while, still with no sign of the kids coming in, the lights would be turned back on to reveal all four boys still on the rink, leaning on their sticks, patiently waiting. As soon as the lights came on, the game would resume.

Eric was the first to leave home, in 2000, when he joined the Peterborough Petes of the Ontario Hockey League. Three years later, Marc departed for the Sudbury Wolves of the OHL, and the following year, Jordan followed in his oldest brother's footsteps, joining the Petes. Finally, it was Jared's turn, and he played with Sudbury.

First junior, then pro. After two solid years with the Petes, Eric made the jump to the NHL at eighteen, the first pick (second overall) of the Carolina Hurricanes in 2003. While he would enjoy a very good rookie season, scoring 11 goals and 31 points in 81 games, Eric admitted he went to training camp thinking it would simply be a good learning experience.

"I wasn't expecting to make the team," Eric said. "I was going in with my eyes wide open, but I really didn't know what would happen. I just wanted to see where I fit in. When I first got to Carolina, it wasn't like I was expecting to stay. Once I got to camp and started practising and got into a few exhibition games, I started to feel more comfortable. I scored a few goals in the exhibition games, which helped my confidence."

It was clear to anybody who watched Eric competing against his older and more experienced competition that this kid was special. At six-foot-three and 200 pounds, he was physically ready to make the jump. But was he mature enough?

"It was really weird initially," he said. "I was a lot younger than the next youngest guy on the team who, I think, was twenty-six. We had a lot of older guys who had been around and had played in the league for a long time, but they were really good with me. That made it easier for me. I remember playing in my first exhibition game and skating on a line with Ron Francis, whom I'd grown up watching on TV. It was pretty surreal."

Eric's impressive play through the pre-season prompted the Hurricanes to keep him and he nearly scored in his first NHL game.

"We were in Florida, and Ron Francis gave me a pass from the corner," he said. "I went blocker [side] high on Roberto Luongo and I hit the knob of his stick. I still remember that chance today. I was seeing that one in my dreams that night. Fortunately, a couple of games later, I got it done."

It was Carolina's sixth game of the year, a 2–0 win over the Bruins in Boston. After going pointless in his first five games, Staal cashed in big time against the Bruins, scoring the winning goal and assisting on the insurance marker. On his first goal, he got help from a teammate who also came from a hockey family. Jeff O'Neill, whose brothers Don and Ryan both played in the OHL, made a great play to set up Eric.

"I was on a two-on-one with Jeff," Eric said. "We busted in together from the red line. O'Neill had a great shot, and he really, really sold the shot and pumped their goalie, Andrew Raycroft, out of the net. He then slid a real hard pass over to me. I stopped it, took a look at the net, and knew I had the whole empty net to shoot at. I was thinking, 'Don't miss the net. You'd better not screw this up, because you don't know how often these empty nets come around.' Raycroft was diving back, but he couldn't get across fast enough."

Eric Staal, who spent the summer convinced he'd be returning to Peterborough for a third year of junior hockey, had his first NHL goal. He very quickly ascended to a leadership role on the hockey team and took over from veteran Rod Brind'Amour as captain of the Hurricanes in January 2010. Those who watched him lead the team in playoff scoring in 2005–06, when the Hurricanes won the Stanley Cup, knew it was only a matter of time before the 'Canes became his team.

Having blazed a trail for his younger brothers, Eric tried to influence them by being a good role model. While Marc was next in line in terms of age, it was actually Jordan who surprised people by becoming the second brother to make the NHL. The second-overall pick by the Penguins in the 2006 NHL Entry Draft, Jordan went to his first NHL training camp hoping, like Eric, to live and learn.

"I was not worried about making the team or not; I just wanted to show them what I could do," Jordan said. "I knew I was a young guy, and I knew if I made the team it would be unbelievable, but it wouldn't really be expected, and if I didn't make the team, I'd just be going through what a lot of kids go through who get sent back to junior. If that happened, hopefully I'd make it the following year. I went out and had fun and just showed them what I could do.

"My rookie camp was pretty solid. I was pretty nervous, but in the exhibition games I was okay. They kept me around and gave me an opportunity. The biggest thing is, they kept me on the team, and once the season started, I was so jacked up about being with the Penguins I started to play very well."

As a centre, no matter how well Staal played, the best he could hope for was to be third on the Penguins' depth chart. That's because he had two superstar centres, Sidney Crosby and Evgeni Malkin, playing ahead of him. Nevertheless, Jordan quickly made his mark in the NHL as a dependable defensive centre who could supply his team with valuable offence from the No. 3 slot.

He scored his first NHL goal in the centre of the universe, New York City—an unassisted marker made possible after he stole the puck from one of the best players in the NHL.

"It was against the New York Rangers in Madison Square Garden," Jordan said. "There's no better place to get your first NHL goal. There's no bigger stage than New York City. It was my first time in New York. It was a shorthanded goal, which was pretty neat. I picked off Jaromir Jagr's pass, and then I flipped the puck past one of their defencemen and ended up on a breakaway. I put it over the blocker of Henrik Lundqvist, and it was a pretty amazing feeling.

"When you break in alone, you're living in your own world. You're not really thinking a whole lot. The hockey senses just sort of take over. You just do what comes naturally to you. Even now, when I talk about it, it gives me chills. It's an unbelievable feeling—something a player will never forget. It's a moment in hockey that is one of the best, if not the very best."

Scoring while his team was killing a penalty became something of a specialty for Jordan, who used his breakaway speed to catch his opponents flatfooted. In fact, his first three NHL goals, and 7 of the 29 he scored in his rookie season, came while his team was playing shorthanded.

Like Eric, Jordan would experience the glory of winning the Stanley Cup early in his career. In 2008–09, just his third season in the NHL, Jordan helped Pittsburgh defeat the Detroit Red Wings in seven games in the final. The victory came one year and eight days after the Penguins lost to the same Wings in six games in the final.

Jordan was fortunate to have an older brother in the league to offer him advice. Eric was extremely proud that his brother was getting his name engraved on the Cup. In a rare moment of candour, Eric let a little secret about Jordan out of the bag.

"I remember talking to Jordan a lot before he went to his first camp with Pittsburgh," Eric said. "I was eighteen, turning nineteen, at my first camp, but Jordan was eighteen and wasn't turning nineteen for nearly a year, so he was really young going to his first camp. I remember telling him to work as hard as he can, but to remember this is the NHL and to make sure he had fun and play loose."

Jordan took his brother's words perhaps a little too close to heart. Play loose? How about playing your whole rookie season in skates that were too big?

"He played the whole year in skates that were a full size too big," Eric said. "I remember the next year, he was trying to figure out his skates because he was having problems with them, and I asked him what he wore the year before. He said, 'They figured out my skates were a full size too big last year.' I said, 'Why did you do that?' He said, "Hey, I was in the NHL. I was living the dream. Whatever they gave me, I just put on my feet and wore.' I could not believe that he said that. I was laughing, but he was dead serious."

Marc Staal was a junior star from the get-go, but his development was a little bit slower than his brothers. It took him until the ripe old age of twenty to make the NHL. The brothers' competitive nature came out in those backyard scrimmages, so it should come as no surprise that Marc, who was drafted twelfth overall by the New York Rangers in 2005, was affected by Jordan making the NHL before he did.

"I was sent back to Sudbury by the Rangers, and Jordan made Pittsburgh," Marc recalled. "It was a little bit weird for me to be still be playing junior and watching him play on TV with the Penguins. After a while, though, I realized I was sent back to junior for a reason, and that was to work on my game. The fact that Jordan was already in the NHL ended up motivating me to work harder on my game so I could get there, too. We ended up having a great year in Sudbury, making it to the OHL final, so it was probably my best year in terms of development."

If Marc was thrilled at the notion of being drafted by the Rangers, one of the NHL's highest-profile teams, his mom, Linda, wasn't nearly as excited. From Thunder Bay to Broadway?

"My mom said when I was up on stage putting on the Rangers jersey, she was sick to her stomach with fear," Marc said. "New York City is so huge compared to Thunder Bay. I have to admit it took a while for me to get used to."

It was in the Rangers' eighteenth game of the season, a 4–2 win over the rival New Jersey Devils, that Marc finally got his first goal, which was assisted by veterans Scott Gomez and Brendan Shanahan.

"Gomer had the puck in the corner and Shanny was standing in the slot," Marc said. "Gomer made the pass, and I am certain it was meant for Shanny, but he let it go back to the point, where I was standing. I moved in and I remember thinking to myself, 'Just blast it as hard and high as you can toward the top elbow of the net.' That is exactly what I did, and it beat Brodeur over his shoulder.

"I actually wasn't really sure if I had scored or not. One of our wingers, Sean Avery, was standing in front of the net, and I wondered if he tipped it. Then I saw the guys all skating toward me, and I knew I had the goal. It was a pretty amazing feeling."

Like the rest of his family, Marc Staal is pretty laid back. Still, he admitted that the fact his first NHL goal was scored against Martin Brodeur was significant.

"It will probably mean a lot more to me twenty or thirty years from now, knowing my first NHL goal was scored against a Hall of Famer," he said.

Jared turned pro in 2010–11 in the ECHL, one of the lower rungs of the professional hockey ladder, but had graduated to the American Hockey League, one level below the NHL. Having scored in both of those leagues, he is still chasing that first elusive NHL goal.

COLIN AND GREGORY CAMPBELL

JANUARY 19, 1975 (COLIN)
NOVEMBER 15, 2005 (GREGORY)

WHEN YOUR DAD IS THE TOWN'S SHERIFF, there are those who will accuse you of getting an easy ride. Nobody knows this better than Gregory Campbell, whose father, Colin, became the NHL's senior vice-president and director of hockey operations. One of the main duties for a man in his position is to dole out discipline when players act up—a job that makes anyone holding the position highly unpopular with the masses.

For Gregory, following in his father's footsteps as an NHL player, the fallout was inevitable. Thankfully, he's a thick-skinned lad whose dad taught him well to ignore other's ignorance, especially those who thought his path to the big leagues had been paved by his father.

"It's never been really bad," Gregory said. "I think probably if people do say things, it's behind my back. People may have their opinions about me if they don't know me, but if you were to ask anybody who has played with me in junior or the NHL, they would say I deserve to be where I am and I have worked for everything I have gotten. It bothers me if people think I only got to this level because of who my dad is, because I have worked so hard. I would like the respect I deserve for being Gregory Campbell, not Colin Campbell's son."

Colin was a rugged stay-at-home defenceman who spent a year in the World Hockey Association followed by eleven years in the NHL. He then went on to a coaching career, and was behind the New York Ranger bench, assisting Mike Keenan, in 1994, when the Rangers won their first Stanley Cup in fifty-four years. He takes great pride in his son's ability to handle his detractors.

"I think in the early years, he used to take some chaffing," Colin said. "It started in junior. He took a little bit of chaffing in junior when I was coaching the Rangers and he was playing in New York. It really started to take effect in junior, but he got pretty good with his comebacks. One player once said to him, 'The only reason you're here is because of your old man,' and that hurt him. He fought the guy. In the NHL, guys have laid off for the most part."

Besides, Colin insisted, there is a huge upside to having your dad play and coach professional hockey. That, he insists, is what drove his son to become a pro hockey player like his dad.

"I think the fact some kids grow up in the game, they love the game and they are so exposed to it, it helps if they want to play pro," Colin said. "They have the internal drive, because their dad did it and they want to do it. They are in a hockey family and they map out all the things that they have to do to make it to the NHL and they try to emulate their fathers. I don't know if it's so much a case that their talent is significantly better than other kids, but they have been in a hockey atmosphere and the drive is there."

Colin didn't have that luxury. He grew up in the small tobacco-producing town of Tillsonburg, Ontario, and moved away at seventeen to play junior hockey with the Peterborough Petes, where he played under, and then became a lifelong friend of, legendary coach Roger Neilson. In his final year of junior, 1972–73, he put up decent numbers—7 goals and 47 points in 60 games—but it was his toughness and 189 penalty minutes that attracted pro scouts. Colin was drafted in the first round, fifth overall, by the Vancouver Blazers of the WHA and second round, twenty-seventh overall, by the Pittsburgh Penguins of the NHL. He joined the Blazers and played in the inferior pro league for one year.

"The WHA was like a glorified American league," he said. "It was actually great when you look back and realize you got to play against guys like Gordie Howe, Bobby Hull, and Andre Lacroix. The trouble is, it was one tough, mean league. All the goons who couldn't make the NHL played in the WHA. You didn't have three extra players sitting out every game like we do now in the NHL. If guys were hurt or suspended, you'd play under the roster maximum. You just went with what you had. Some nights, you'd have sixteen or seventeen players [instead of twenty]. I used to put Vaseline in my hair, because guys would grab your hair from behind or from the bench when you were fighting. You had to be ready. It was like a street fight. It was a tough, tough league."

The next season, he signed with Vancouver, but started the year in the AHL with the Hershey Bears. It was there that he met Bob McManama, who would be instrumental in his career. Colin Campbell was never mistaken for a high-end puck-rushing defenceman, so it was decidedly uncharacteristic for him to jump into the play the way he did when he scored both his first AHL and NHL goals.

"When you think about a guy like Bobby Orr, you'd imagine his first goal being an end-to-end rush," Colin said. "And a guy like me, who didn't score much? Well, mine was an end-to-end rush. My first goal in Hershey was a shorthanded breakaway goal assisted by Bob McManama. My first goal in the NHL was a shorthanded breakaway was a shorthanded goal assisted by Bob McManama. It was on Ron Low, and I have a picture of it. Don't ask me how I got a picture of it. Nowadays, you have pictures of just about everything players do, but back then that wasn't the case. I have a picture of me skating past the net and Ron Low digging the puck out of it."

So, how does a defence-minded blueliner find himself on a breakaway while killing a penalty?

"Don't ask me—I just jumped into the play," Colin said with a laugh. "You can see in the picture I have that I am skating out from the goal line and my teammates are skating toward me to congratulate me, so it is obvious I was in all alone."

And that's not all.

"Believe it or not, my first NHL playoff goal was a shorthanded breakaway assisted by Bob McManama," Colin insisted. "I used to wonder if this was just a story that had grown in my own mind over the years, but I went into one of the offices where we have all the old issues of *The Hockey News* and I checked it out, and it was true. Bob McManama was my roommate and didn't play too much, but he assisted on those three goals."

Sadly for Campbell, McManama only played 99 NHL games, scoring 11 goals and 36 points. He played in just eight playoff games, and his only point was that assist on Campbell's first post-season tally. Who knows: if he had played longer, perhaps Campbell would have won the Norris Trophy. Or a scoring championship.

Gregory had the good fortune of growing up at the rink. Just about every day was take-your-son-to-work day. There was never really any doubt that he'd play pro hockey, too.

"I was cleaning up one day, and I saw a couple of pages that Gregory had written on when he was young," Colin said. "He had written the names Steve Yzerman and Adam Graves and Wayne Gretzky on a piece of paper. He knew Wayne from New York, where I coached. He wrote, 'Win one for the Gipper' and his favourite movie: *Rudy*. He had also written, 'I want to win the Stanley Cup so bad I can taste it.' He was ten years old, living in Rye, New York. I took that note paper and I framed it, along with some pictures of him playing hockey in Rye, as well as pictures of him playing for the Kitchener Rangers and Florida Panthers.

"Gregory was a rink rat. He was always around the rink and often travelled with the team. I remember we were on a plane after having been beat out of the playoffs by Philadelphia. It was actually the last playoff game that Gretzky and Messier played together. So Gretzky comes up to Gregory on the plane and says, 'Peaks and valleys, Gregory. Peaks and valleys.' Gregory was twelve at the time. Any time he has a tough time, I remind him, 'Remember what Wayne said: "Peaks and valleys."'"

Looking back, Gregory said he was blessed to have the opportunity to rub shoulders with many great players. He didn't get to see his dad play pro, but he certainly had a front-row seat for many years when his dad coached in Detroit and New York.

"For me, it was all I knew," Gregory said. "Other kids would ask questions and think it was so cool—which I did, too. I didn't overlook the fact I got to hang out in an NHL locker room every day. From the day I was born, it was just natural to me. It was a part of my life, but also something I enjoyed. Obviously, there was never any pressure to play hockey, but the more I enjoyed it, the more I continued to play it. I had the benefit of always being around that atmosphere. I also had the luxury of sitting in on team meetings. I would be floating around or hanging around the medical room and just soaking in everything I could, kind of like a fly on the wall. It got to the point where, as years went on, people didn't even realize I was there because I was there so often. For a regular kid to see Mark Messier and Wayne Gretzky every day would be amazing, but to me it was just an everyday part of my life—not that I took it for granted. It was just normal. It was all I knew."

Gregory Campbell also played junior hockey, with the Plymouth Whalers and Kitchener Rangers. He was a dependable and gritty two-way centre who blossomed in the spring of 2003, when he helped Kitchener win the Memorial Cup. After scoring 23 goals and 56 points in 55 regular-season games, Gregory fired 15 goals and 19 points in 21 OHL playoff games.

Gregory started his first year in the American league, but was recalled by the Florida Panthers, who had drafted him in the third round in 2003.

"It was two weeks into the season when I got called up from San Antonio," Gregory said. "The Panthers never really got a good look at me at my first training camp because I blew my MCL [medial collateral ligament of the knee] out in my first rookie game. I was just hanging out and rehabbing for about a month and a half before being sent to the AHL. Then they recalled me to give me a taste of what it was like to play in the NHL. With [Mike] Keenan being the coach, I didn't last too long. He liked older guys."

It wasn't until the following season that he would score his first NHL goal. It was Florida's nineteenth game of the season, and it was in Montreal, arguably the most exciting place to play hockey in the world.

"Montreal is my favourite place in the league to play, and I think that also goes for a lot of guys," Gregory said. "It is such an amazing atmosphere. The stands are filled in warmup. People are so alive there; they know the game. The way the arena is built, you feel like the fans are right on top of you.

"We were down 3–0 going into the third, and I was having a pretty good game. I scored lots of my goals on the way up, especially in junior, on deflections, and that is how I got my first NHL goal. It was on a shot from our defenceman Eric Cairns. I was in the high slot area when he took his shot. I was even with the faceoff dot and I tipped it on my backhand. It bounced once and went over the goalie's glove.

"I still watch that goal from time to time, and you can see a big smile on my face. I was shocked that it went in. At the time, I was fighting for my job still, so it was a very happy moment. It was funny that Eric got the assist on my first goal, because when he played for my dad on the Rangers, I used to sit in the family room with him and Ryan VandenBussche during the games when they were healthy scratches. Next thing I know, I'm playing on the same team as him."

Was that Gregory's best memory? Perhaps. However, he has one that certainly rivals it.

When Gretzky retired, Colin Campbell was given the equipment the Great One wore in his final game and was asked to deliver it to the Hockey Hall of Fame in Toronto. Campbell brought the equipment home to Tillsonburg for a few days, where his son stumbled upon it.

"I don't know if Wayne knows about this," Gregory said. "I found the box with Wayne's equipment, and I just took it upon myself to throw on the helmet. The next thing you know, I was dressed head to toe in all of Wayne's equipment.

Everything except the skates. I'm certain that not too many people who look at that exhibit at the Hall of Fame are aware that I was the last guy to wear it."

COLIN AND CAREY WILSON

MARCH 1, 1984 (CAREY)
OCTOBER 21, 2009 (COLIN)

COLIN WILSON KNEW THE GOAL would come eventually. All he
needed was a little help from his friends. When the 2008 first-
round pick of the Nashville Predators went pointless in his
first four NHL games, he wasn't too worried. Wilson had
been on the road to success since he was a teenager playing
in the United States National Team Development Program,
and some would argue he was predisposed to play professional hockey, following in the footsteps of his father, Carey,
who enjoyed a productive ten-year NHL career with the
Calgary Flames, Hartford Whalers, and New York Rangers.

Nobody was expecting instant miracles from Colin
Wilson, although, since the Predators had traditionally been
a low-scoring outfit prior to his arrival, it was hoped he
would eventually help boost the offence. At six-foot-one and
215 pounds, he was big, strong, and fast.

Wilson suggested that a more perfect scenario could not
have been written for his first NHL goal.

"I saw the schedule, and we were going to be playing our
fifth game of the year in Boston, and I was extremely excited
about that," said the Greenwich, Connecticut, native who
was coming off playing two years with the Boston University
Terriers. "As soon as we got off the plane, I went straight to

the university campus to visit my college buddies. I went to watch their hockey game, and when it ended, Coach [Jack] Parker called me into his office and gave me my championship ring. I was very happy to get that."

It was while playing with the Terriers that Wilson confirmed for most hockey scouts that he was definitely NHL material. He was named the ECAC rookie of the year, the fifth player from Boston University to earn the honour, after scoring 13 goals and 35 points in 37 games in his freshman year, 2007–08. The year before he joined the Predators, he bumped his numbers up to 17 goals and a league-leading 38 assists for 55 points. No one was surprised when he passed on his final two years of school to turn pro.

Wilson was delighted to see his old teammates play that Friday night, and was even more thrilled that many of them came to watch him play against the Bruins the following day.

"The next night I got ten or twelve of the guys tickets for our game against the Bruins, and sure enough I scored my first NHL goal with the guys in the stands," he said. "It was really exciting to have them there.

"I had some good chances to score in my first four games. I knew it would come eventually. The thing is, it took me nine games in college to score my first goal, and also, when I went to play for the American national team, it took me eight games to score. I'm kind of used to it taking a while to get that first goal."

Wilson was anxious and excited at the same time as he stepped onto the ice in Boston. He saw his pals in the stands and was determined to send them home happy.

"Patrice Bergeron of the Bruins had the puck in our defensive zone, and I pushed him off the puck and gave it to Patric Hornqvist, who was standing at the side boards,"

Wilson recalled. "We skated into the Bruins zone, and he ripped a shot on net that their goalie, Tim Thomas, saved. I was going hard to the net and saw the puck lying on the goal line. I beat Derek Morris to the puck and just pushed it across the line.

"It was definitely a relief, and a stepping stone in my career. I tend to put a lot of pressure on myself, and when it takes that long to score, the pressure just keeps on building. Once I got it, I knew I would score more. It was just a matter of getting that first one."

Colin laughs at the fact it took him five games to score his first NHL goal, because his dad got his first goal on his second shift in the league.

Like Colin, Carey Wilson also took the college route to the NHL, playing two years at Dartmouth College before taking an unusual bend in the road, joining HIFK Helsinki in the Finnish Elite League for two seasons.

"Education was always very important to me," Carey Wilson said, "and at that stage of my life, I really didn't think I was going to wind up playing professional hockey. My first year at Dartmouth was a great experience. I think we finished in the top three. The next year, though, it was like going from the penthouse to the outhouse. We didn't make the playoffs. One of the things I really needed to work on was my skating, and I figured playing pro in Finland on the big ice surface over there would help me. I also knew, because their seasons started and ended early, I could return to Dartmouth to finish my degree."

He stuck to the plan, and then, in 1983–84, joined the Canadian men's national team to prepare for the 1984 Olympic Games. The team, which included future NHLers Patrick Flatley, Dave Gagner, Dave Tippett, James Patrick,

Bruce Driver, Russ Courtnall, Kirk Muller, and J.J. Daigneault, among others, played together for an entire season prior to the Games in Sarajevo, Yugoslavia. Although the team was made up of mostly youngsters, it would not enjoy the same success at the famous USA "Miracle on Ice" team from four years earlier. Canada finished fourth in the tournament, which was won by the powerful Soviet Union, a team that featured superstars Vladislav Tretiak, Slava Fetisov, Vladimir Krutov, Igor Larionov, and Sergei Makarov.

Canada finished second in the B Group, with a 4–1 record, outscoring its opponents 24–10. In the medal round, however, their youth and inexperience became apparent. Canada finished 0–3 and was outscored 10–0. Still, Wilson has nothing but good memories of the year.

"As a group, we faced a lot of adversity with the travel and players coming in and out of the lineup," Wilson said. "Some of the guys went on to great careers in the NHL, and for me it was a great opportunity to play with those guys. It was a season for us. It wasn't like it is today, where they get together for a couple of weeks and play a tournament. We played the whole year together—played in tournaments in Europe. As I look back on it now, it is something I cherish and look back on as a great opportunity."

Following the Olympics, Carey Wilson joined the Calgary Flames for the final sixteen games of the regular season and the playoffs. Unlike his son, Carey had instant success.

"On my first shift, I leaped over the boards, and suddenly I noticed all the people in the stands getting to their feet and cheering," Carey said. "It took me a few seconds to figure out they were cheering for me. I would have liked to have scored a goal on my first shift, which I didn't, but it was pretty unbelievable to get a standing ovation."

He was stunned by the instant acceptance of the fans. He endeared himself to the locals on his next shift when he scored. Wilson admits it wasn't the prettiest goal of the 169 he scored in his career, but it was memorable nevertheless.

"I would like to say I picked up the puck behind my own net, skated through the entire team, and even deked a couple of guys twice before roofing a shot past their goaltender, but that's not the way it happened," Carey said. "I actually got the puck, and as I was skating into the Flyers zone, I saw their two big defencemen right in front of me. One was Brad McCrimmon, who had a butt that was about half the width of the rink. I knew I had to get the puck past him, so I lowered my head and fired at shot at the goal. It wasn't exactly a laser. In fact, I think it went end over end, but it somehow got past their goalie, Bob Froese. It was a borderline dump-in shot just to get rid of the puck before I got cranked. I think McCrimmon was just about to stand me up."

Carey said when it came to advising his son, he kept the message pretty simple: have fun.

"I tell him to enjoy it," Carey said. "Nobody puts more pressure on elite athletes than themselves. I know my son is like that, and I was like that, too. You have to do it with a smile on your face and really take the time to enjoy what you are doing along the way."

FRANK AND PETER MAHOVLICH

MARCH 24, 1957 (FRANK)
NOVEMBER 6, 1966 (PETER)

YOU'D HAVE TO GO A LONG WAY to find brothers who played such drastically different styles of hockey than the Mahovliches, Frank and Peter. Frank, the Big M, was a hulking, yet graceful left winger with a powerful stride and booming slapshot. He typically played a calm game, although you didn't want to wake the beast because, although he had a long wick, when he got mad, look out! Frank was one of the most prolific scoring wingers in NHL history.

Peter, lightheartedly referred to as the Little M, even though he stood four inches taller than his older brother, was a gangly, energetic centre who took a long time to find his game as a pro, but ultimately developed into a fine two-way performer and a tough, physical player.

Here's another difference: Frank remembers scoring his first NHL goal as if it was yesterday, while Peter recalls the circumstances, but darned if he just can't remember exactly how he got his. That's okay, though, because Peter does recall vividly scoring the goal that many consider to be one of the prettiest ever scored, in game two of the famous 1972 Summit Series between Canada and the Soviet Union.

Frank Mahovlich was destined to be a star in the NHL. When he was just seventeen years old, he was the second-leading scorer on the Toronto St. Michael's Majors of the Ontario Hockey Association, with 24 goals and 50 points in just 30 games in 1955–56, and everybody knew it was just a matter of time before the Toronto Maple Leafs summoned him for an audition. Late in the year, with the Leafs destined to miss the playoffs, he was called up to the NHL for the Leafs' final three games.

"My first practice in the NHL was Ted [Teeder] Kennedy's very last practice in the NHL," Frank said. "It was a thrill for me to be on the ice with him. I skated by him, and I remember him cursing at me. He was quite a competitor. I ended up replacing him the following season."

When it finally came time to play with the Maple Leafs, Frank found himself in something of an unfamiliar position.

"Howie Meeker, who was our coach and general manager, asked me to play a defensive role in my first game," Mahovlich said. "We were playing the Montreal Canadiens, who had won five straight Stanley Cups, so they were pretty good, and I was asked to check Maurice Richard. I can remember their best defenceman, Doug Harvey, had the puck at the blue line, and I was standing beside the Rocket at the red line, keeping an eye on him. Harvey passed him the puck and he started to take off. I panicked and put both arms around him. I was young enough at the time, or maybe just a little stupid, and I said, 'You're not going anywhere.' I was a fairly strong guy. He turned toward me, and his eyes were staring at me and he said, 'Let go, kid!' I said, 'Yes, Mr. Richard.' He didn't score in that game, but we lost 2–1."

The Leafs also lost in Frank's second big-league game, at home to the Detroit Red Wings, but he made his mark in game three in Detroit.

"I was playing centre in that game, and I came down my wrong side, the right wing," Frank said. "I was a left-handed shooter skating in on the right side. I let a shot go just over the blue line that beat their goalie, Glenn Hall. It was a floater that went through a couple of defencemen and went clean into the net. It was a good goal, but I don't think Hall saw the puck."

The following season, Mahovlich joined the NHL on a permanent basis and quickly established himself as a rising star in the league. The same year, another young left winger named Bobby Hull also broke into the NHL, with the Chicago Blackhawks. While Hull arguably had a higher profile, it was the Big M who won the Calder Trophy as the NHL's rookie of the year, scoring 20 goals and 36 points in 67 games, compared to Hull's 13 goals and 47 points in 70 games.

Incredibly, Frank Mahovlich and Hull almost became teammates when the Blackhawks offered Toronto $1 million for Frank, who was involved in a contract dispute with the Leafs. Frank ultimately re-signed with Toronto, but his career took him to Detroit and Montreal in the NHL as well as Toronto and Birmingham in the World Hockey Association.

He won six Stanley Cups (four with Toronto and two with Montreal) and was inducted into the Hockey Hall of Fame in 1981. Like many of the game's best players, Frank saved his greatest hockey for the playoffs, and in 1970–71, his first Cup year with the Canadiens, he was particularly efficient, scoring 14 goals and 27 points in 20 games. That was the year the Habs called up rookie goaltender Ken Dryden, and he shocked the hockey world by winning the Conn Smythe Trophy as playoff MVP.

"A lot of people look at that Cup year and give most of the credit to Dryden," said hockey historian Dick Irvin. "Dryden was amazing, but I can tell you the Canadiens would not have won the Cup without Mahovlich. He was actually the Canadiens' best player in the playoffs that year."

After his retirement, Frank Mahovlich was appointed a senator by Prime Minister Jean Chretien in 1998. Looking back on his fine career, Frank laughs when he recalls his first NHL goal against Hall. As it turned out, it wouldn't be the final time he victimized the great stopper, although the two became good friends.

"I never knew Glenn had a bit of a lisp when he spoke," Mahovlich said. "I was at his induction into the Hockey Hall of Fame, and when I introduced my son Michael to Glenn, I said, 'You know, Glenn, I scored my first NHL goal against you.' Then I told him I also scored my first NHL hat trick against him—in Chicago, December 1, 1957. He said, 'You *bathtard!*' That's when I found out he had a lisp."

Being the younger brother of an established NHL superstar could present problems, but that was never the case for Peter Mahovlich. In fact, he credits his family, particularly his older brother, with helping him make it to the NHL.

"Everybody talked about pressure, but I didn't feel that internally because there was never any pressure put on me at home about me being a hockey player or being like my brother," Peter said. "It was more about making sure I got an education, and if I ended up being a hockey player, that would be fine. Of course, Frank was so supportive of whatever I wanted to do. He always said to me, 'You're going to be your own hockey player. I don't expect you to be like me. Just play the way you want to play.' If you have pressure from the outside world and then you have pressure at home, too, that could really crush you."

Unlike Frank, there were no guarantees Peter would make it to the NHL. Based on his play as a junior with the

Hamilton Red Wings, he was probably a long shot at best, yet he was persistent, and his hard work and dedication ultimately paid off. The second pick in the 1963 amateur draft, Peter was a gangly centre best known for his ability to check. As he became more comfortable with his stature, he would ultimately develop into a dependable point producer, too, but when he first was called up to the NHL by Detroit, in 1965–66, it remained a mystery as to exactly what type of player he was.

After Hamilton's season concluded, Detroit called Peter up for two more games, and the following season he turned pro and reported to the Pittsburgh Hornets of the American Hockey League.

"I still had a year of junior eligibility, but the Red Wings figured I had learned as much as I could at that level," Peter said. "I played seven or eight NHL pre-season games and scored four or five goals. It helped the fact that I played on a line with Gordie Howe and Alex Delvecchio."

Peter split the season between Pittsburgh and Detroit. Although he doesn't recall the exact circumstances of his first NHL goal, scored November 6, 1966, in a 6–0 win over the Montreal Canadiens, he does remember being particularly pleased with scoring against the Habs.

"I know most players remember their first goals vividly, but I don't," Peter said with a laugh. "What I do recall, however, is it was extra satisfying because Montreal had the first pick in the draft and took Garry Monahan, and I was the second player chosen, so it was great to score against the team that passed on me in the draft."

Peter bounced back and forth between the NHL and the minor leagues his first four seasons as a pro, but finally hit his stride in 1970–71 with, of all teams, the Montreal Canadiens.

He had been traded to Montreal for—you guessed it—Garry Monahan. After having scored 9 goals and 17 points in 36 games with the Canadiens in 1969–70, Peter took his game to the next level the following year, connecting for 35 goals and 61 points with 181 penalty minutes in 78 games. Frank Mahovlich's younger brother had finally arrived!

"Back then, we didn't do a lot of off-ice conditioning," Peter said. "As I got older, I started paying closer attention to conditioning and diet," Peter said. "I probably didn't become physically mature until I was twenty-two or twenty-three years old. I also had a lot of knee problems when I was young—never anything serious, just nagging injuries. It was a slow transition for me, but I honestly believed I was going to make it one day. If you look at what I did in Fort Worth in the Central Pro league, I averaged more than a point per game. Then I would get to Detroit and I wouldn't play that much. You needed to play more—as a big person, it was tough sitting on the bench for long stretches. In Montreal, my playing time increased and my confidence grew."

Peter ultimately became a key member of four Stanley Cup championship teams with the Canadiens. More important, when the NHL gathered its best players for the legendary Summit Series against the Soviet Union, Peter and Frank were both included. Peter dressed for seven of the eight games and managed one goal—but what a goal it was!

Team Canada was shocked by the Soviets, 7–3, in the series opener in Montreal on September 2, 1972, a night many Canadians will never forget—for all the wrong reasons. Two nights later, the teams gathered again in Toronto, and Canada bounced back, thanks in a large part to the Mahovlich brothers. Peter scored what has been described by some as the most beautiful goal ever scored.

"It still gives me chills thinking about it," Peter said. "Your chest just swells up with pride. What set it up was how badly we were beaten in the first game after taking a 2–0 lead. In the second game, we knew how good they were on the power play and we got up 2–0. We were killing a penalty when they scored a goal. Suddenly, our two-goal lead was down to one goal, and then right away we take another penalty. I'm sitting beside Phil Esposito on the bench, and he says to me, 'If we get the puck, we have to rag it. We have to control the puck when we get it and don't give it up.'

"Sure enough, I got the puck, and as I'm getting to the centre line I'm thinking that I'm going to fake a shot and then turn back toward my team's end and hold the puck for as long as I could. That was my first intention. It wasn't to beat their defenceman, Yuri Liapkin. As I got to the defenceman, I faked my shot and he got right on his tippy-toes. I quickly realized that I could get by him, so I drove to the net, made the move on Vladislav Tretiak, and scored."

Frank scored his only goal of the series two minutes and twelve seconds later to give Canada a 4–2 win. The Mahovlich brothers, though different in personality and playing style, helped save the day for a hockey-mad nation.

CHRIS AND SEAN PRONGER

NOVEMBER 6, 1993 (CHRIS)
JANUARY 25, 1997 (SEAN)

WHEN YOU GET TO KNOW THE Pronger brothers, Sean and Chris, it is obvious that they share a lot of similarities.

The Dryden, Ontario, natives are both tall and lanky, both are great hockey players, and both of them have a wonderful sense of humour. Chris is the more celebrated of the two, and when he holds court with reporters in a media scrum, it can be wildly entertaining.

But there are obvious differences, too.

Chris, who is six foot six and 220 pounds and is two years younger than Sean, is one of the toughest, most intimidating and feared defencemen ever to skate in the NHL. He was once suspended for stepping on Vancouver Canucks forward Ryan Kesler. The more mild-mannered Sean, a self-professed journeyman, had undeniable skill, but in his ten years as a professional hockey player, he was never able to stay with one team for a long period of time. He was too good for the American Hockey League, but not quite polished enough to make his mark in the NHL.

Chris insisted his reputation is often blown out of proportion, although there would be a long line of his opponents who have paid the price after going up against him who would beg to differ.

"It's all reputation," he said with a laugh. "You get suspended a few times early in your career and you get a reputation. Do I cross-check guys? Yes, I do. But I don't do anything that other players don't do, too. I get speared, I get cheap shots, and I don't hear anybody talking about that."

While Sean acknowledges his brother's nasty nature, he said that those who dislike his younger sibling often overlook the most important aspect of his game.

"There is no question Chris is one of the most intense players in the game," Sean said. "But I don't know if it's his intensity that intimidates opponents as much as it is his will. He will literally outwill the opposition. And not only does he break the other team, he has the ability to will his team on."

While Chris never takes prisoners when he's on the ice, his older brother never felt his wrath.

"Chances are if I was out there, he was probably not on the ice or just leaving the ice," Sean said. "His teams played him against my team's top lines, which I was rarely on. There were a few times when we crossed paths, but there was never a steady match-up. I think there was one time when he could have taken my head off, but he let me off the hook. I knew as soon as he came up on me he could have nailed me, but he just gave me a whack. Other than that, we really didn't have a whole lot of interaction on the ice."

The brothers are close, but actually only played one season as teammates when they were in peewee.

"They changed the age groupings, so instead of moving up to bantam, I stayed in peewee and we played together," Sean recalled. "It was fun. I think we have great chemistry when we play together. Even in charity games, we seem to click. Mind you, it's a much slower pace, which is right in my wheelhouse. We have a similar thought process, so I think we would have played well together if we had been on the same team in pro."

One distinct difference between the Pronger boys was the route they took to make it to the NHL. While Sean quietly played four years in the NCAA with Bowling Green, Chris was a high-profile junior superstar with the Peterborough Petes of the Ontario Hockey League.

After first informing OHL teams he would follow his brother to an American university, Chris Pronger changed his mind and decided to play for the Petes, who took a big chance by drafting him in the sixth round. Chris was an instant star in junior hockey, scoring 17 goals and 62 points in 63 games as a rookie, and then 15 goals and 77 points in 61 games as a sophomore. Even more impressive, he helped the Petes make it to the Memorial Cup final that year, scoring 15 goals and 40 points in 21 playoff games.

When the NHL draft rolled around, there was a glut of highly rated players who might have gone first overall, but the Ottawa Senators settled on Alexandre Daigle, while the Hartford Whalers chose Chris with the second pick. Upon being chosen, Daigle said, "I'm glad I got drafted first, because nobody remembers Number 2." Incidentally, Daigle was a bust, while Pronger went on to win the Hart Trophy as the NHL's most valuable player and the Norris Trophy as the league's top defenceman and helped the Anaheim Ducks with the Stanley Cup in 2006–07. He also played on two gold medal–winning teams at the Olympics.

Chris joined the Whalers for the 1993–94 season, and right away he was identified as a special player. Although he was quite lean in his rookie year, there was no changing his game.

"You have to have the mentality that I had—the same one I have had my whole career," Chris said. "You don't back down, you don't give an inch. Back then there were some big guys who were 230, 240, and 250. You have to know how to move guys. You learn little tricks. In junior, I wasn't the biggest guy, either, but I learned how to manage guys like that.

"I had a meeting, prior to my draft, with the San Jose Sharks, and right off the bat, they told me they weren't going to draft me. One of the questions was, 'If Eric Lindros is standing in front of the net, how would you move him?' I said, 'I'll just poke him in the back of the knee and push him away from the net.' I think they were expecting me to say I wouldn't be able to move him.

"You have to play the way you know how. You don't alter your game just because you reached a new level. The first couple of years I was in the league, we played Boston eight times a year, so I got to watch Ray Bourque. I watched the way he contained guys. There was one game he played thirty-eight minutes. It was pretty impressive."

Chris managed 5 goals and 30 points with 113 penalty minutes in his rookie campaign. Not a bad statistical line for a nineteen-year-old, but not really an indication of the offensive force he would become. His first NHL goal came against the New York Islanders, in his fifteenth game.

"It was a nice little snap shot that found its way through traffic and went through the goalie's five-hole," Chris said. "We were on the power play when the puck came back to me at the point. I knew the goalie was screened, so I let a wrist shot go. There was always another part of the dream that I was chasing. I wanted to get drafted, and then I wanted to play in the NHL, and then I wanted to score in the NHL, and then I wanted to win a Stanley Cup in the NHL. There's always that next part of the dream that you are chasing, that you want to fulfill. Obviously, scoring your first NHL goal is one of the bigger ones."

Sean, meanwhile, turned pro a year after his younger brother and split his first season between San Diego of the International Hockey League and Greensboro and Knoxville of the East Coast Hockey League. He had been drafted in the third round, fifty-first overall, in 1991 by the Vancouver Canucks, but elected to stay in university to get his degree. Smaller by three inches and lighter by about ten pounds, Sean played centre and hoped to make it as a goal scorer. Suffice it to say, he saw a different side of professional hockey than Chris, who was in "the apple."

Sean got his first taste of the NHL the following year, when he skated in seven games with the Anaheim Ducks. He drew one assist, but spent the majority of the season working on his game with Baltimore of the AHL. The next year, he finally made his mark in the NHL.

"I was having a great year offensively in the minors and got called up from Baltimore in January," Sean said. "No one was hurt at this point, so I knew if I was going to stick with the Ducks, this was my big chance and I had to make the most of it. I knew if I played well, there was a spot for me. I put a lot of pressure on myself, and I was playing well, but I wasn't producing. I played five games and didn't score, but I played decently.

"Jack Ferraro, who was the general manager, pulled me aside after a game during a road trip, and I'm thinking, 'Oh no, I'm being sent back down.' I've been pulled aside before, and the news was never good. But this time, he said, 'Sean, I want you to get your stuff sent here from Baltimore and go get yourself a place to live for the rest of the year.' I was stunned. I thought the opposite was going to happen. At that point, the pressure came off me, and I scored in the next game against Los Angeles, in Los Angeles."

Sean recalled his first of the 23 goals he would score in the NHL.

"It was off a rebound," he said. "I was playing on a line with our team's two best players, Teemu Selanne and Paul Kariya, and there was a shot on net. I was standing between the hash marks and the puck came to me. I fired it at the net, and it went under the goalie, Byron Dafoe.

"As soon as it went in, I wondered, 'Did it count? Did the whistle blow? Are they going to wave it off?' I scored a million goals in my dreams, and something always went wrong. But this one counted.

"The feeling was not one of excitement, but actually one of relief. It was like, 'Finally!' I had so many chances, and I knew I had to do something to stay up. Once I was told I was staying, I was so much more relaxed. The next game was in St. Louis, and I scored in that game. I think I ended up scoring four goals in four games. After that, I thought to myself, 'I might score 50.'"

There were to be no 50-goal seasons in his future, not even in the minors or Europe, where Sean finished his career.

Nevertheless, both Pronger boys managed to play in the best league in the world, and after scoring their first NHL goals, shipped the pucks back home to mom and dad in Dryden. Their parents still have the souvenir pucks.

SIX

MEMORABLE MOMENTS
AND WINNING STORIES

Previous page: Paul Henderson scored 236 goals in his NHL career, but will always be most remembered for scoring the game winner of the '72 Summit Series. (Getty Images)

PAUL HENDERSON

JANUARY 29, 1964

WHEN SIDNEY CROSBY SCORED the gold medal–winning goal for
Canada in overtime against the United States at the 2010
Winter Olympics in Vancouver, nobody was really surprised.
Crosby, after all, was the face of the Canadian team, and even
though he was only twenty-two years old, he was considered
by many to be the best hockey player on the planet. The
expectation was that if Canada was to be successful at the
Olympic hockey tournament, Sid the Kid would likely have
a hand in its victory. He didn't disappoint.

The same cannot be said for Paul Henderson, who scored
the biggest goal in the history of the sport on September 28,
1972. Until that day, Henderson was regarded as a slightly
above average player, strong on both sides of the puck, but
nothing really out of the ordinary. Prior to his own personal
miracle on ice, Henderson had accumulated 187 goals and
375 points in 568 NHL games with the Detroit Red Wings
and Toronto Maple Leafs—decent numbers, to be sure, but
again, not close to the top producing forwards of the day.

Henderson had been a highly productive junior star for
the Hamilton Red Wings, scoring 49 goals in 48 games in his
final year in the Ontario Hockey Association. The Red Wings,
like many junior clubs, were sponsored by the NHL's Detroit
Red Wings, and once each season the big-league club would

make the short bus trip to the southern Ontario city of Hamilton to play an exhibition game against the juniors.

"It was a big deal for us," Henderson said. "The [Detroit] Red Wings would come to Hamilton and play, and then we'd all go out, the two teams, after the game. A few years later, I was coming back with Detroit to play in Hamilton with the Detroit team, so I was on the other side of the fence. It was really a lot of fun."

Of course, the fans loved it, too. It was a wonderful opportunity to see their NHL heroes, the likes of Gordie Howe, Alex Delvecchio, and Red Kelly, up close and personal. Back then, there wasn't nearly the television exposure of hockey that we have today. It was also a time when the parent team would often call up junior-aged players as emergency replacements for injured NHLers. So it really wasn't so unusual that Henderson was summoned to Detroit near the end of the 1962–63 season.

"Hamilton had been beat out of the playoffs and I hadn't been on skates for about eight days," Henderson said. "I remember wishing that I had been able to skate a bit more leading up to my first NHL game. As it turned out, it didn't really matter. My dad drove me to Detroit, and on the way to the game he told me I should do something to make an impression. So, on my first shift, I dropped my gloves and fought Toronto's Dick Duff."

Henderson wasn't known as a fighter, even as a junior, but he decided nonetheless to follow his father's advice, and dropping the gloves was his way of being noticed. He laughs about it now.

"I looked around for the smallest guy I could find, I chopped him a good one with my stick, and then we fought," he said. "It turned out to be the only shift I got in the game."

Henderson survived his NHL debut, and even made a name for himself. And he wasn't done yet.

"The next game was in Toronto, and the coach, Sid Abel, told me to keep a close eye on Frank Mahovlich," Henderson recalled. "On my first shift, I was out with Frank, and he started to get away from me, so I slashed him. He went down in a heap and then jumped up, threw his gloves off, and wanted to fight me. The officials got between us, and Frank is yelling, 'Let us go! Let us fight!' I am thinking to myself, 'No bloody way! Stay between us!'

"Once again, it was the only shift I got in the game. So you look at my NHL record from that season, and it shows two games, no goals, no assists, and no points, with nine penalty minutes. And I got those nine penalty minutes in about ten seconds of ice time spread over two games."

His first NHL goal would have to wait.

Henderson went to Detroit's training camp at the start of next season, but didn't feel he was ready to play in the NHL. He knew he would be one day, but for now he was determined to find his legs as a pro before trying to play full time in the best league in the world. He thought he would be better served playing for Detroit's American Hockey League affiliate in Pittsburgh.

"The older guys in Pittsburgh really helped me. We were leading the league, and I was getting lots of ice time. Midway through the year, the Red Wings insisted I come up to Detroit, but I basically got only one or two shifts a period. It was awful and I hated it. The next year, I got to play a lot more, and after that, it was fine. But even in the second year, I was on the third line and didn't get a whole lot of ice time. By my third year I played regularly."

Upon being recalled from the minors, where he had 10 goals and 24 points in 38 games with the Hornets, Henderson did whatever was asked of him. He was used to being more of a go-to player on his previous teams, but with the Red Wings, he had to wait his turn. The team featured stars such as Howe, Delvecchio, Norm Ullman, Marcel Pronovost, and goalies Roger Crozier and Terry Sawchuk. Although he wasn't convinced he belonged there, he knew he would do whatever he could to help his new team.

"It was around Christmastime when I got called up," Henderson said. "I didn't score right away, but that was okay. I knew I'd score eventually. All they had to do was give me some ice time and I knew I'd score. But when you are only getting one or two shifts a period, you had to be very conscious of not letting your guy score. You thought primarily defence. You didn't want to be a liability. I knew the offence would come."

It took a while, but Henderson finally got the elusive first goal.

"We were in Chicago, and I was playing on a line with Pit Martin and Parker MacDonald," Henderson said. "Pit and I skated into the Chicago zone, and he passed the puck to me. I went around their defenceman, Moose Vasko, and fired a shot high over the shoulder of Glenn Hall.

"It's funny . . . you dream about scoring your first goal, and then when you get it, you move right on to the next game and you try to score again. It wasn't that big a deal."

Perhaps it is not such a big deal now, especially after having scored the biggest goal in the history of the sport, but he collected the puck regardless.

"I dug into the net and grabbed the puck, but don't ask me where it is now," Henderson said. "I haven't got a clue where it is. I wasn't really big on saving things from my career. I wish I had been now. I did save the pucks from my 100th and 200th goals, though."

Henderson ultimately developed into a very good NHL right winger, and after nearly five seasons with the Red Wings was part of a major trade with the Maple Leafs that brought Mahovlich to Motown. Henderson wasn't a surprise addition to Team Canada, but nobody expected him to be the hero of the international event. In fact, he was put on a checking line with Maple Leafs teammate Ron Ellis and a rising star from the Philadelphia Flyers, Bobby Clarke.

That all changed when Henderson took it upon himself to signal a teammate off the ice in the final minute of game eight and then stormed to the front of the Soviet Union's goal, where he slammed the puck past a startled Vladislav Tretiak. As everybody in Canada held their collective breath, legendary announcer Foster Hewitt called the action: "Here's a shot . . . Henderson made a wild stab for it and fell. Here's another shot . . . right in front . . . They score! Henderson has scored for Canada!"

In an instant, Henderson became a national hero. The fact he had scored the game-winning goals in games six and seven only served to heighten the majesty of his colossal accomplishment.

There has been an ongoing debate as to whether or not Henderson should be inducted into the Hockey Hall of Fame based on his performance at the Summit Series. For the record, Henderson doesn't feel he did enough to be inducted. He told the *Toronto Sun*: "If I was on the committee I wouldn't vote for myself. I don't think I deserve to be in. I did not have a Hall of Fame career. I had a wonderful series in '72 with a great bunch of guys, but there's a lot of players [more deserving] . . . I never made the first or second all-star team, I never won a major trophy, so I have no problem with not being a member whatsoever. Quite frankly, I'm very comfortable with who I am and with what I've accomplished."

Henderson will always be remembered for scoring the Summit Series winner, but it all started with a shot over the shoulder of Hall of Famer Glenn Hall.

KEN MORROW

IF KEN MORROW HAD NEVER PLAYED a single game in the NHL, he could rest comfortably at night knowing he was a big part of what many consider the greatest sporting achievement of all time: the Miracle on Ice.

For the majority of players on the 1980 gold medal–winning Team USA, it was the crowing achievement of their hockey careers. For Morrow, however, it was only the beginning of what was to be one of the most spectacular seasons ever enjoyed by any player. Not only did he earn a place in history by helping the United States beat the powerful Soviet Union en route to capturing gold in Lake Placid, he then joined the New York Islanders and became the first player in hockey history to win a gold medal and the Stanley Cup in the same season.

Looking back, Morrow said his life was a whirlwind at the time and he didn't really grasp what he actually experienced until years had passed.

"It definitely comes later in life," Morrow said. "Things were happening so fast for me. In the course of a week, I won an Olympic gold medal, participated in my first practice with the Islanders, and played in my first NHL game. The game was six days after we won the gold medal. It was happening fast and furious. I think it was a good thing that I didn't have time to sit down and think about it."

Morrow went from being a part of one of the most tight-knit, well-coached hockey teams in the history of the sport—a team of destiny—to joining one of the NHL's most celebrated dynasties. The Islanders were in the initial stages of what would be a four-year run as Stanley Cup champs, and Morrow arrived just in time to enjoy the ride.

"It was surreal," Morrow said. "I had watched these guys for years. I had been drafted by the Islanders in 1976, but I didn't really know any of them. I had watched them on TV, watched this team turn into one of the best teams in the league. My biggest concern was, how was I going to win a job and play on this team?"

Selected in the fourth round, sixty-eighth overall, in the 1976 amateur draft, Morrow had never even attended a training camp with the Islanders before joining them late in the 1979–80 season. With Denis Potvin, Bryan Trottier, Mike Bossy, and Battlin' Billy Smith, the club's dynamic goaltender, leading the way, the Islanders were just hitting their stride as one of the most dominant NHL teams of all time. Quiet by nature, Morrow blended into the background initially and simply allowed his game to do his talking.

"I had met the coach, Al Arbour, and GM, Bill Torrey, but the first time I walked into the room for practice was the first time I had actually met the guys," Morrow said. "The guys were great. I truly believe that team had so many great, character players. On top of being Hall of Fame players, one of the reasons why that team had so much success was because they had so many players with character. When I walked into the room, they made me feel right at home. A lot of them came up to me and said they had watched the Olympics on TV and they were cheering for us at home. They made me feel at ease.

"It wasn't so much chasing a Stanley Cup; it was more about trying to earn a job and stay with the team. I didn't know originally if I was going to Long Island or to the Islanders' farm team in Indianapolis. Torrey had told me I was coming to Long Island right away, and I was thrilled. It was a matter of jumping right into the fire right away."

Morrow played in the final eighteen regular-season games with New York, quickly establishing himself as a safe, stay-at-home defender whose size and toughness were valuable commodities on a team that already boasted equal portions of skill and depth. He came in on a high, having just won the gold medal, but he still had to earn a spot, for as much as what he had accomplished at the Olympics, the Islanders were on a different mission.

"Looking back, they wanted to see if I could play or not, because the trade deadline was just a couple of weeks away," Morrow said. "My first game was against the Detroit Red Wings at Nassau County Coliseum, and it just happened to coincide with the return of defenceman Denis Potvin, who had been out for more than half the year with a thumb injury. He had missed forty games, and his first game back was my first game. It was almost like they had two new players coming into the lineup at the same time.

"The only thing I recall is how the game ended. We were down by a goal, and Mike Bossy scored at the buzzer and they disallowed the goal. We lost by a goal. My second game was the next day in Pittsburgh, and we tied the Penguins."

Morrow said if he had any scoring opportunities in those first eighteen games, he doesn't recall them. He did register three assists, but none of those have been committed to memory.

"All I remember is the team went on a winning streak at the end of the year," Morrow said. "We made the trade with the Los Angeles Kings to get Butch Goring [for Dave Lewis and Billy Harris], and right after Butch joined the team, we went on a twelve-game unbeaten streak. The team got on a roll and we were able to carry that into the playoffs,"

By time the playoffs rolled around, the twenty-two-year-old Morrow had established himself as a regular on the Islanders blue line along with the likes of Potvin, his brother Jean Potvin, Stefan Persson, Dave Lewis, rugged Gord Lane. And with the playoffs came Morrow's first NHL goal.

Typical of the way things were going for Morrow at the time, it wasn't just any goal, it was an overtime winner. The two teams split the first two games of their best-of-five series on Long Island before heading to Los Angeles. The Kings, comfortable in their home surroundings, jumped into a quick 3–0 lead in game three, and the Islanders, favoured to win the series by many, were suddenly in deep trouble.

That was until young grinder Alex McKendry, who had scored just twice in twenty-two games with the Islanders during the regular season, chipped in a pair as New York tied it 3–3. If McKendry was an unlikely goal scorer—his two goals that day were the only two NHL playoff goals of his rather short big-league career—then Morrow's heroics certainly came out of nowhere.

"The goal, actually, was like a lot of my goals," Morrow said. "It was a typical Ken Morrow goal in that the puck went into their end while I was on the bench. Whoever was on defence for us at the time came over for a change, so I jumped over the boards and skated to my point position at the right point. As soon as I got there, just inside the blue line, the puck came back to me and I took one of those half-slappers right along the ice. It was going about ten feet wide, but it hit the skate of one of their defenders who had one of my teammates covered, and bounced behind Mario Lessard in their net.

"I saw the puck go in, and I was just as surprised as everybody else. With my shot, I wasn't one of those guys who was going to be beating goalies too often with blasts from the point. My biggest thing was just trying to get the puck through and on net. This one was going wide, but I was fortunate it hit a skate and surprised Lessard."

The Islanders were alive and well thanks to Ken Morrow's first NHL goal. New York defeated Los Angeles in four games, and then went on to eliminate the Boston Bruins and Buffalo Sabres to earn a trip to the Stanley Cup final and a meeting with the Philadelphia Flyers. The Islanders beat the Flyers in a hard-fought six-game series that culminated with Bob Nystrom scoring the Cup-winning goal in over-time on May 24, 1980.

"Winning the Cup was almost relief," Morrow said. "It is such a grind and survival of the fittest. Some people say the Stanley Cup is the hardest trophy to win in all of profes-sional sports, and there's no doubt in my mind that it is. It's two months of playing nearly every other day. You beat one team, and then you have a tougher team waiting for you in the next series. All you have to do is look down the bench and see the looks on the faces of the guys when you get to the final. Everyone is exhausted and covered in bruises . . . not to mention being ten, fifteen, or twenty pounds lighter than what they started the year at. My one memory of being in the final that first year was walking up the steps at Nassau Coliseum to get to your car after the morning skate. As the playoffs went on, it was actually a chore to walk up those two flights of stairs. That's how tired your legs were."

Although other players have since played for Olympic and Stanley Cup champions in the same year, Morrow was the first to pull off the feat. He still gets chills when he thinks about what he accomplished.

"They were both unexpected and both lifetime thrills," Morrow said. "In three months, I played in the Olympics, won the gold medal, played in my first NHL game, scored my first NHL goal, and won the Stanley Cup. I was very lucky, and I'm thankful for it all."

Morrow was a defensive specialist who wound up scoring 17 goals and 105 points in 550 career games, and another 11 goals and 33 points in 127 Stanley Cup playoff games. He didn't score often, but when he did, he made his goals count.

"I ended up scoring three overtime goals out of the eleven career playoff goals I had," Morrow recalled. "I didn't score a lot of goals, but I had some pretty memorable ones."

JIM VESEY

AL IAFRATE ONCE BROKE IN ALONE on an empty net and, rather than scoring a goal, he deliberately fired a shot wide of the gaping cage. Asked afterwards why he passed up on an easy score, the Toronto Maple Leafs defenceman said he didn't feel it was honorable to score into an empty net.

Guess it was easy for Iafrate to be flippant. Aside from being one of the most eccentric players ever to skate in the NHL, the Harley-riding defenceman—who is said to have worn his hockey helmet in the shower because he was convinced it helped prevent hair loss—scored 152 goals in 799 career games. The fact of the matter is, Iafrate actually scored just one empty-netter in his career: on February 18, 1992, for Washington against San Jose.

Now, Jim Vesey, a natural and consistent goal scorer at every level he played at, scored a grand total of one goal in his short and otherwise nondescript fifteen-game NHL career. And wouldn't you know it, he scored into an empty net.

"It's weird," Vesey said. "You always dream about your first goal being a beautiful goal. Nobody grows up dreaming their first NHL goal will be an empty-netter—especially if you had never scored before. Why the heck would they even have you out there with an empty net if you had never scored before?"

Well, the Blues did have Vesey on the ice late in the game while protecting a lead against the Toronto Maple Leafs, and the big centre took advantage of his opportunity. And he scored a goal he'll never forget.

"We were playing in Toronto, and I was playing on a line with Bernie Federko and Rick Meagher," Vesey recalled. "In that game, I also had an assist, but just getting the opportunity to play with those guys was great. Usually when I got called up, they put me with the likes of [enforcers] Craig Coxe and Dave Richter."

That's the way it was in those days. When teams were short-staffed, they'd often call up the best scorer from their minor-league affiliate. But rather than put the player on a line with other scorers, they'd play them just a few shifts per game with role players, which is a polite way of saying slugs. Teams generally didn't want to upset the chemistry of the players who had been with the team all season by inserting a newcomer into a position that commanded a lot of ice time.

Indeed, Federko and Meagher were two of the Blues more skilled players—in particular Federko, who was named to the Hockey Hall of Fame in 2002. And Vesey sure wasn't about to pass up on such a great opportunity.

"Late in the game, we were up by a goal and my line was on the ice," Vesey said. "It actually felt pretty good knowing they trusted me in that situation. Toronto pulled its goalie and we were pressing in their zone. I passed to Federko, who took a shot, but missed. The puck went into the corner where Rick got it. I was cutting to the net from the high slot and Rick spotted me. He passed to me and I put it into the empty net."

Vesey's only NHL goal may not be one for the ages, but he certainly earned the right to play in the NHL. The Charlestown, Massachusetts, native knew his way around the net. Drafted in the eighth round of the 1984 NHL Entry Draft, 155th overall, Vesey was a scoring star with Merrimack College, firing a whopping 40 goals and 95 points in 40 games. And he was no shrinking violet, either. As well as leading his team in goals and points, Vesey also led his team in penalty minutes with 95.

So it was no surprise he made a rather seamless transition to the pro ranks, leading the Peoria Rivermen of the International Hockey League in scoring with 47 goals and 93 points in 1988–89. Surely the NHL would soon be his next destination.

It was that season when he got his first call to the show, and Vesey didn't waste the opportunity. In five games with the Blues, in addition to scoring he assisted on another goal and engaged in his only NHL fight. The next season, though, it was back to the IHL, where he again scored a team-high 47 goals and was second in points with 91. His reward? Another half-dozen games with the Blues, in which he registered one assist—his final NHL point, as it turned out. He was up for various stretches with the Blues, but spent most of the time in the press box as a healthy scratch.

Vesey's professional career would last another five seasons, mostly in the minors, where he continued to produce at a very high level, piling up numbers that should have gained him more attention from NHL teams. It just wasn't in the cards. It was frustrating at the time, though he has come to grips with his place in the hockey world.

"There were a lot of guys who got even less opportunity than I did, but when you look at my stats, my first year in the IHL, I was an all-star along with Mark Recchi and Theo Fleury," Vesey said. "Both of those guys went on to be NHL stars. I'd get called up to the Blues, and there was Brett Hull and Paul MacLean ahead of me at right wing on the depth chart. I put up huge numbers in the minors, but when I got called up to the Blues, I wasn't really put in a position to put up points.

"The knock against me was my skating, but I remember as a kid watching Charlie Simmer, who wasn't a great skater, and when they put him with Marcel Dionne and Dave Taylor, he was able to succeed. If you put me with good linemates, I scored goals. I played with Michel Mongeau and Nelson Emerson in the minors and put up big numbers. I produced in college and the minors, and all I ever wanted was a 20-game opportunity with some good linemates at the NHL level. I knew if I ever got that chance, I could produce. Instead, I'd get four or five shifts a game with fourth-line grinders.

"I was never given a chance where they said to me, 'Here's a spot for you and it's up to you to lose it.' I tell people now, you can't score in high school or college hockey playing three shifts a game."

After helping the Rivermen win the Turner Cup in 1990–91, Vesey was traded to the Winnipeg Jets. However, his mother suffered a stroke, and Vesey wanted to be closer to home, so he requested another trade.

"Winnipeg GM Mike Smith, whom I had never met before, knew I was a Boston guy," Vesey said. "I told him I didn't want to play in Winnipeg and that I wanted to be close to my mom in Boston. I felt I had paid my dues, and apparently he agreed. They traded me to Boston and I was assigned to the Maine Mariners of the American Hockey League. I played on a line with Andy Brickley and Nevin Markwart, two skilled guys, and I had 6 goals and 13 points in 10 games."

That earned him a trip back up to the NHL with the

Bruins. Vesey was convinced this was his golden opportunity. Again, however, it was to end in disappointment.

"I got the opportunity play the power play with Ray Bourque, and I just had a feeling I was going to score," Vesey said. "We were playing at the Boston Garden and I took a pass from Bobby Carpenter and was nailed in the neutral zone by Steven Finn of the Quebec Nordiques. The pass was in my skates, but instead of bailing out, like I probably should have, I wanted to show them I wasn't afraid of being hit. When I got the puck, my whole right shoulder was exposed, and when Finn hit me, my right arm went up and over and the whole joint of my shoulder popped out. I suffered a lot of nerve damage and had to have major shoulder surgery."

He had a second shoulder surgery while playing for the Phoenix Roadrunners of the IHL two years later. The injury had a lingering affect on Vesey's game and he wasn't able to do the things he was used to. It ultimately led to him retiring at the age of thirty, his dream of becoming a big-time NHL goal scorer put to rest.

"The game had stopped being fun. Because of my shoulder problems, I really didn't enjoy playing anymore," he said. "Most of my goals were scored from in front of the net, where you paid a price. You also had to stick up for yourself. Wearing the brace, I couldn't do anything. When people start taking liberties with you and you can't protect yourself, it's hard. I hated playing."

Lest you think Vesey's NHL empty-netter was the height of his goal-scoring creativity, he actually scored a few memorable goals in his career. The one that sticks in his mind the most came the year he helped lead the Rivermen to the Turner Cup title.

"It was against Mario [Goose] Gosselin of the Phoenix Roadrunners," Vesey said. "Our coach, Bob Plager, had scouted Phoenix and told us, 'Don't shoot at Gosselin's glove side; he has a great glove.' We were on a five-on-five in their building when I got the puck and I roofed the puck top shelf, glove side. In the dressing room after the game, they made a video highlight of the goal and everybody was saying, 'Don't go for his glove side! Bobby Plager says he has a great glove.' We all laughed. Whenever we get together, guys still show that tape and say, 'Don't shoot at his glove.'"

Oh, and by the way, if empty-net goals are not honorable, somebody forgot to tell Wayne Gretzky. The NHL's all-time leading goal-scorer had 55 in his illustrious career.

SCOTT HOWSON

JANUARY 22, 1985

GIVEN THE UNBELIEVABLE START TO his NHL career, it's hard to imagine we don't speak of Scott Howson in the same breath as we do such snipers as Wayne Gretzky, Rocket Richard, Mike Bossy, and Brett Hull. After all, it isn't every player who steps into the National Hockey League and scores goals on their first four shots. That's right: four shots, four goals.

Unfortunately, as gifted a scorer as Howson was—we're talking about a player who scored 57 goals in his final year of junior and then bagged another 57 in his first season of pro—the party didn't last. In fact, Howson played in just 18 NHL games over two seasons and completed his big-league career with 5 goals and 8 points.

Howson had the good fortune to be signed as a free agent by the New York Islanders after being passed over in the draft, but as it turned out, there was a logjam at centre. While he was lighting it up in the minors, the Islanders were coming off four straight Stanley Cup championship seasons and had the likes of Bryan Trottier, Pat LaFontaine, Bob Bourne, Butch Goring, Brent Sutter, and John Tonelli, among others, playing ahead of him.

Howson, who was on the smallish side at five-foot-eleven and 160 pounds, got his pro career off to a wonderful start when he fired 55 goals and 120 points for the Toledo

Goaldiggers en route to being named rookie of the year in the International Hockey League. The Toronto native continued to be a minor-league scoring star with Indianapolis of the Central Hockey League, where he had back-to-back seasons of 34 goals, but still he didn't get a sniff from the Islanders. His chance came the following season, when he was recalled by New York to fill in during a spate of injuries.

"The Islanders had so many injuries, I got to play right away," Howson said. "They were so decimated with injuries, and because it was 1985, the Islanders were at the end of their fantastic run and the team was a little bit older."

After toiling in the minors for nearly four years, Howson finally hit NHL ice on January 22, 1985, against the Detroit Red Wings. It didn't take him long to net his first NHL goal.

"It came in the first period," Howson recalled. "I was on a long two-on-one with Bob Nystrom. I think I got the puck around our blue line and we broke in together—me on the left side and Bob on the right side. The defenceman stayed in the middle, so I kept the puck. I went to my backhand and took a quick shot that appeared to get caught up in the equipment of their goaltender, Corrado Micalef. I didn't know it went in until I circled past the net. It was a thrill for me to be first of all on the ice with that team, but then to get that first NHL goal.

"I have a great shot from the paper the following day of Nystrom and I celebrating the goal. Nystrom is congratulating me. His face is facing the camera, and you can tell by the look on his face he is so excited for me. It was a great memory. The funny thing is, I walked out of the rink the next day and a fan came up to me with four pictures of the goal. The fan had taken snapshots in sequence of me shooting the puck, going behind the net and looking, and then me raising my arms in celebration, so I have two really wonderful mementoes of the goal."

"For me, it was more about playing in my first NHL game than it was scoring the first NHL goal," Howson said. "The first game is such a thrill. It's a thrill for the puck to go in, for sure, but just being on the ice was amazing. I was so nervous before the game, I felt like a little kid. On my first shift, I went into the corner for the puck against Detroit's Brad Park. I thought, 'What's going to happen here?' He gave me a push and I stayed on my feet and I thought, 'Okay, I can do this.' That probably gave me as much confidence as anything. I remember that moment distinctly. I mean, here's Brad Park, a superstar who has been in the league twenty years, and I went in and battled with him and survived."

Not only survived, but excelled. Howson wasn't done with his first goal. He scored another in the game, giving him two goals on two shots.

"That was more of a quick shot from the slot," Howson said. "I got the puck and quickly whipped it in."

Sadly, the Islanders lost the game 5–4, but they returned to action two nights later, when they hosted the Toronto Maple Leafs.

"That was a much bigger deal for me," Howson said. "I was born in Toronto, and I knew the game was being televised back home and that my family and friends would be watching. The score was 2–1 for us, and for pretty much all of the game, our coach, Al Arbour, had kept me away from their top scorers, Rick Vaive and Dan Daoust. We were playing four on four and I was out with Clark Gillies, and I headed to the bench expecting Al to take me off, but he left me out and I ended up getting a goal on a slapshot that went high over their goalie Tim Bernhardt's shoulder to make it 3–1 and to seal the game for us."

Make it three goals on three shots. Surely his teammates must have started giving him the business.

"Actually, I don't remember them doing that," Howson said. "I do remember Al coming up to me after practice following the first game and saying offhandedly, 'There's nothing to this game, huh Scott?'"

Howson made it a perfect four for four in a Saturday afternoon game on Long Island with the Washington Capitals in town. The Islanders lost 5–1, but Howson connected "on a bang-bang pass play in front of the net, and I just banged it past Pat Riggin."

Rather than think how easy it has been to score goals so far in his brief NHL career, Howson actually thought about how lucky he was.

"My first game, I played on a line with Nystrom and Duane Sutter," Howson said. "How good is that? How many guys get a chance to play on a line like that right away? The next game, I got an assist against the Minnesota North Stars, but eventually the injured players started coming back and I started getting less ice time. Eventually, I was scratched and then I got sent back down."

After five years of playing professional hockey, mostly in the minors, Howson decided it was time to move on. He completed his university education and then got his law degree. He worked at a Toronto law firm, but longed to get back into the game, and after a couple of years he was hired by the Oilers. Howson served as the general manager of Edmonton's American Hockey League affiliate—the Cape Breton Oilers, and then the Hamilton Bulldogs—before becoming the Oilers' assistant GM in 2002. He held that position until June 15, 2007, when he was named general manager of the NHL's Columbus Blue Jackets.

He got to live his dream. Scott Howson played in the NHL, albeit for a short time, and he scored eight goals. It was getting to play in the league that he treasures the most.

DEAN MORTON

OCTOBER 5, 1989

JUST ABOUT EVERY CANADIAN BOY who has ever laced up skates dreams of playing in the NHL and Dean Morton is certainly no exception. Unlike most, however, Morton's dream actually came true.

A big, tough defenceman at six-foot-one and 200 pounds, Morton not only made the Detroit Red Wings out of training camp in 1989–90, he scored a goal in the team's season opener in Calgary. Sweet!

It's not fair to say that Morton's dream quickly turned into a nightmare, because he actually enjoyed a respectable five-year professional career, winning championships in the American and Colonial leagues. But after scoring that goal in a 10–7 loss to the Flames, Morton never again skated in the NHL.

The native of Peterborough, Ontario, remained with the Red Wings for the rest of the western road swing, but was a healthy scratch for games in Vancouver and Los Angeles. When the team returned to Detroit, he was dispatched to the minors, where he remained until he hung up the blades following the 1992–93 season.

Sad story? Not so fast.

Morton never lost his desire to return to the league, and he actually made it happen—as a referee. That's right: the one-time bad boy who racked up 767 penalty minutes as a pro made it back to the NHL in 1999–2000 as an official responsible for keeping the peace.

After helping the Adirondack Red Wings win the AHL championship in his first season of professional hockey in 1988–89, Morton arrived at Detroit's training camp the following September, his third pro training camp, determined to take the next step in his career.

Morton was never much of a scorer in junior with Ottawa and Oshawa of the Ontario Hockey League, but he could play a very physical game. Every hockey player loves to score goals, but the truth of the matter is that hitting and fighting were more Morton's thing. This time, he had a game plan: he was going to make his mark physically, even though he understood his chances of making the Red Wings were still a long shot.

"When I went to that training camp, I was never mentioned as anybody who would be in serious contention to make the top eight," said Morton, who was twenty-one years old at the time. "I knew I still had to prove myself. I didn't have any expectations beyond going out and enjoying camp and simply doing the best that I could. Things really rolled for me in camp. I had a couple of really good open-ice hits, and I think that opened a few people's eyes. I also moved the puck pretty well."

When the exhibition games rolled around, Morton continued to impress. He dished out a monster hit on Toronto Maple Leafs veteran Eddie Olczyk that sparked a line brawl. In the next game, he crushed another vet, the Minnesota North Stars' Dave Gagner, with a jaw-dropping open-ice hit.

"The local media really seemed to pick up on the fact that I was dishing out these big hits, and I believe I made the team based on what I had done in camp, not because of any advanced publicity or expectations," Morton says. "I was never going to score many goals, but I knew I could make a reputation for myself by hitting."

When the big night arrived, the season opener, Morton was prepared. Based on his forceful physical play in the pre-season, he was included in the lineup for Detroit's first game, in Calgary. Coming off their only Stanley Cup victory, the Flames raised their championship banner prior to the start of the game, and the crowd roared in celebration as the fresh-faced rookie standing on the Red Wings' blue line tried to control the butterflies fluttering in the pit of his stomach.

Once the game started, it was a blur. Before Morton could blink, the Flames had built a 3–0 lead.

"It was awful," Morton said with a laugh. "You just knew the last shot on goal was going to win the game. I think we knew we were in trouble when I scored the first goal of the season for the Red Wings."

With his team trailing, Morton scored the goal of his lifetime.

"We were playing five-on-five, and we had the puck down low in the Calgary zone in the right corner," Morton says. "Steve Yzerman and Marc Habscheid were doing their thing, and all of a sudden the puck came back to me. It was sliding perfectly along the ice, so I didn't stop it. I fired a one-timer low to the far side of the net, and I swear it went through three sets of legs. Calgary's goalie Mike Vernon was screened, and I don't think he ever saw the puck. I did, though. When I saw the puck go in, it was surreal. Actually, the whole game was unreal.

"When the puck went in, I was shocked. Steve Chiasson skated past me and tapped me on the butt with his stick and said, 'Let's keep 'er going.' He had a big grin on his face."

Chiasson and Morton grew up together in Peterborough and were paired together through most of the pre-season. However, in this game, Morton played with veteran Lee Norwood.

Looking back, Morton can't believe how quickly things unfolded in his brief NHL career.

"You think you are really ready for your first NHL game, but it flies by so fast," he says. "I wish I was able to absorb it all, but it just flies by."

The 10–7 loss meant Detroit coach Jacques Demers would make changes for game two. Morton spent the next two games in the press box, fetching hot dogs and popcorn for veterans Borje Salming and John Chabot, who were also healthy scratches.

Morton wasn't the least bit upset when he was sent to Adirondack. On some level, he kind of expected it.

"The experience was good," Morton says. "It wasn't a huge disappointment being sent down, because I figured I was just starting my career and I'd eventually be called back up. A few years later, though, when I was never called up again, it was disappointing."

Morton bounced around the minors for five years, and, when he realized the NHL was out of his grasp, he retired. He wasn't off the ice for long.

Approached by officials in the Ontario Hockey League to consider trying his hand at officiating, Morton was intrigued. He attended an officials' camp in the off-season and instantly decided on a new career path that would keep him in the game he loved. Not only that, it gave him a second chance of making it to the NHL.

"The guys running the OHL took a liking to me because I had played in the league and also played pro, I could skate, and I had a good feel for the game," Morton says. "I also had good size. But the truth is, when I started, I couldn't ref to save my life. I had no idea about what I was supposed to be doing. But they took me on regardless."

Morton started off as a linesman, but quickly accepted the red armbands of a referee. And after a few years in junior, the NHL came calling, asking if he'd be interested in joining their trainee program. Of course he would! Before he knew it, he was back in the NHL.

He immediately noticed some similarities between being a referee and being a player in the NHL.

"You step on the ice as a team of four, and there are high expectations on all four of you to do a good job," Morton says. "In the NHL, there are twenty players on a team, and you can get lost in the shuffle. The first five or ten minutes, all I tried to do was make sure I was in the right place and not getting in the way of the players. A little while later, I saw my cousin, Steve Webb of the New York Islanders, get laid out with a monster hit. We always laugh about that."

After a few years bouncing back and forth between the AHL and NHL, Morton logged his first full big-league season in 2008–09.

"I love being on the ice, being fully involved in the game," he said. "You get an adrenaline rush. I love being in that four-hour bubble . . . We challenge ourselves to be perfect, which will never happen, but we have to strive to be. The NHL is the greatest league in the world, and I'm glad to be a part of it. I love everything about it—except the travel. It's tough being away from my family."

His NHL playing career was not a long one, but Morton now enjoys a great perspective on how things unfolded for him. He's actually kind of proud that he is one of only four players who scored a goal in their only NHL game. Raymie Skilton was the first, when he scored in his only game with the Montreal Wanderers in 1917–18. Rolly Huard did it in 1930–31 with the Toronto Maple Leafs, and Brad Fast scored in his only NHL game with the Carolina Hurricanes, in 2003–04.

"I got my one game, and it was bittersweet," Morton says. "For six or seven years, I wasn't so emphatic when talking about it. I don't know if embarrassed is the right word, but I wasn't thrilled to tell people I only played one game in the NHL, even though I scored a goal. Once I started refereeing, though, I had a better appreciation for what I actually accomplished. I'd be doing a game in the American Hockey League and I'd see guys that had no hope whatsoever of making it to the NHL, and suddenly the fact that I played one game in the NHL didn't seem so bad after all. I'm a little proud of my accomplishment now."

KRIS DRAPER

IN HOCKEY, AS IN MOST THINGS in life, there is a certain order to the way things usually unfold. Crawl, walk, run. Skate, shoot, score. Minor hockey, junior or college hockey, the National Hockey League. You get the idea.

For Kris Draper, though, the deck was shuffled, and he managed to pull off one of the quirkier feats in hockey history by actually scoring a goal in the NHL before he scored one in junior. That's right: while most junior hockey players are dreaming of the day they'll make it to the NHL, Draper played five games for the Winnipeg Jets before taking a step back and playing a season with the Ottawa 67's of the Ontario Hockey League.

In fact, Draper's path to the NHL was about as unorthodox as it gets. It all started when he and his Don Mills Flyers travelled to Calgary in the 1987–88 season to play in the famous Mac's Midget Hockey Tournament. It was there he was spotted by Paul Henry, a scout for the Canadian national team at the time. Calgary just happened to be home to the national program.

Even though he was just sixteen years old, Draper was invited to attend the national team's summer training camp. Of course, it probably helped that he came from a well-known hockey family. His uncle, Dave Draper, coached major junior hockey and was an NHL scout during a wonderful forty-two-year career in the game, while his dad, Mike Draper, played three years at Michigan Tech before embarking on a five-year career as a pro in the minors and finally settling in as a star senior hockey player in Ontario. The game was in Kris Draper's blood.

It was an interesting proposal, and Draper decided "what the heck."

"At the time, I wasn't sure which way I was going to go—the U.S. college route or major junior," Draper said. "This option came up, and I decided to go out there with really no expectations. I just wanted to go and get some experience as a sixteen-year-old kid playing against older, more experienced players. Before I knew it, I was offered a spot with the Olympic program. At the time, it was just after the 1988 Olympics, and I was going to play with the team in hopes of competing in the 1992 Winter Olympic Games in Albertville."

At least that was the plan.

In his first year with the national team, the seventeen-year-old centre managed 11 goals and 26 points in 60 games, playing a solid two-way game that would ultimately become his calling card as a pro. A year later, he scored 12 goals and 34 points in 62 games. With the 1992 Winter Olympics still a few years away, Draper found himself with options where his future was concerned.

Drafted by the Windsor Spitfires of the OHL, his rights were traded to the Dukes of Hamilton, the team that was to host and participate in the 1990 Memorial Cup tournament. Uncle Dave just happened to be the coach of the Dukes. The idea was for Kris to join Hamilton partway through the season and play in the OHL playoffs and the national junior championship tournament. Unfortunately, the Dukes were an abysmal team, and when it became apparent they would not be worthy hosts, they bowed out of the event. Draper never did join the Dukes.

Prior to the following season, having already invested two years with the national team, Draper went looking for assurances he would indeed be a part of the Olympic squad for the Albertville Games. The national team would not oblige him.

"With lots of time left before the next Winter Games, they didn't feel comfortable guaranteeing I would be in the team, and I understood that," Draper said. "They had never done it for anyone before, and they weren't going to start with me. To be honest, I didn't blame them."

Draper had been drafted in the third round of the 1989 NHL Entry Draft by the Winnipeg Jets, who signed him to a contract. The Jets were interested in seeing how he matched up against players in his own age group and suggested he play a season of junior hockey. The Ottawa 67's, coached and managed by the legendary Brian Kilrea, obtained Draper's rights from Hamilton, and it was decided he'd spend the 1990–91 season in the OHL.

Draper was thrilled to attend the 67's training camp and even played a few OHL exhibition games before departing for the Jets' training camp in Saskatoon, Saskatchewan. He said he had no serious expectations of making it to the NHL that season.

"I had a good training camp, and I just thought I'd get a level of experience hanging around the NHL for a bit," he said. "I didn't really expect to make the team, especially the way I got there. I felt like I was off the grid because I had played in the Olympic program and I was going to play my first year in the OHL as a nineteen-year-old. That was where I thought I was going to go. I was 100-per-cent committed to playing the whole year with the Ottawa 67's, but all of a sudden the [Jets'] coach, Bob Murdoch, told me I was going to play in my first NHL game."

Excited beyond belief, Draper made a quick call to his parents, who hopped on the first plane for Winnipeg. It was all unfolding so fast, he didn't have time to take in the magnitude of what was happening to him.

"I remember skating around in warmup, thinking, 'Wow, this is really a dream come true. I'm playing in the NHL.' I'm looking across the centre red line and I see the Toronto Maple Leafs, the team I grew up watching as a kid," Draper said.

The first two periods blew by in a flash, and the Jets built a healthy 6–1 lead. Like most kids in their first big-league game, all Draper wanted was to not look out of place. Just don't screw up! In the third period, he was finding his comfort zone when he followed teammate Pat Elynuik on a rush into the Leafs zone.

"Elynuik coming across the blue line, and he was a right-handed shot," Draper said. "I was cutting behind him, and he dropped the puck for me. I got it at the top of the faceoff circle and I shot it right away. It was basically a knuckleball shot that beat Leafs goalie Jeff Reese. It was the last goal of the game. We beat them 7–1, but I always tell everybody my goal clinched the victory for the Jets. My goal iced the game."

Draper said the biggest thrill was having his parents in the stands watching him in his first NHL game.

"They were such a huge part of everything, and still are to this day," he said. "My dad still comes to fifteen to twenty home games and never misses a playoff game. They are the ones who made the sacrifices, just like so many parents of Canadian kids, making sure they got me to the rink and that I had good skates and good sticks. Even talking about it now, I get chills remembering my parents sitting in the stands for my first NHL goal."

Things never really worked out in Winnipeg for Draper, despite his amazing start with the organization. He wound up being sent back to Ottawa, where he played the year with the 67's and managed to skate in just nineteen more games for the Jets over the next two seasons before being traded to the Detroit Red Wings—believe it or not, for one dollar.

Although he never turned into a goal-scoring machine, Draper did develop into one of the NHL's most effective two-way players, helping the Red Wings win four Stanley Cups. A valuable member of the Red Wings' Grind Line with Kirk Maltby and Darren McCarty, Draper won the Frank J. Selke Trophy as the NHL's best defensive forward in 2003–04, the same season he had a career-high 24 goals.

Along the way, Draper did manage to score a few memorable goals, including the overtime winner in game two of the Stanley Cup final against the Washington Capitals in 1998, as well as a game-winner against the Czech Republic in the semifinal of the World Cup in 2004, in front of friends and family at the Air Canada Centre in Toronto.

"That goal was pretty cool because I was on a team that included stars such as Joe Sakic, Mario Lemieux, and Jarome Iginla," Draper said. "And I had Wayne Gretzky cheering for a goal I just scored."

But the goal he'll never forget came on Thursday, October 4, 1990, against the Leafs in Winnipeg. His first NHL goal.

"I saw the puck go in," Draper said. "I just remember going numb. It all happened so fast . . . from leaving the Olympic program to getting ready to play for the Ottawa 67's, which was something I was really excited about, to going to my first NHL training camp, and then playing in my first NHL game and actually scoring a goal. To this day, the puck is still framed and hanging in my parents' house."

DANNY SYVRET

WHEN YOU THINK ABOUT FENWAY PARK, one of the greatest baseball parks of all time, you generally think about the Red Sox, the Green Monster, and the boys of summer. But a first NHL goal? Not likely.

Danny Syvret certainly didn't grow up dreaming of scoring his first NHL goal in a ballpark, but that is exactly what happened. In his fifth professional season and with his second organization, the talented offensive defenceman made the Philadelphia Flyers out of training camp in 2009–10, felt great about his game and his chances of remaining with the team for the entire year, but then suffered the bitter disappointment of being sent back to the minors, where he had spent the majority of his first four years as a pro.

Suffice it to say, he wasn't too pleased. As much as anything else, Syvret had had January 1, 2010, circled on his calendar. That was the day when his Flyers were to hook up with the Boston Bruins for an afternoon outdoor game, the annual Winter Classic, at Fenway. It promised to be one of the great hockey events of the year.

"I made the Flyers and I felt I was playing pretty well," said Syvret, who was drafted eighty-first overall by the Edmonton Oilers in 2005. "We had an injury on defence, and they called up Oskars Bartulis from the minors. They actually played us together, and we clicked. But then they started to sit me out and kept playing him. I ended up getting sent down.

"I was pretty pissed. I had gotten tickets for the game, and my family had booked flights and hotel rooms. When I went home for Christmas, I told my family to cancel their flights and rooms because I wouldn't play in the game. I had been down in the minors for a month, so what were the odds I'd be called back up for the Winter Classic?"

Pretty good, as it turned out. In Philadelphia's first game back after the Christmas break, defenceman Ryan Parent hurt his back, and Syvret was recalled on December 27. At the last minute, his mom and dad and an uncle drove to the game, while his older brother got a last-minute flight and arrived the day of the game.

"At the time I got called up, Ryan Parent was day to day, so I still wasn't sure I'd play in the game," Syvret said. "I didn't really want to tell my parents to book their flights again, because as soon as I did I could have been sent back down again. And I hadn't been around long enough to be in a position to ask the coach or the GM if I was going to play in the game. I just had to wait and see. If Ryan had taken the morning skate and determined he was okay to play, I would have been shipped back to the minors."

Luckily for Syvret, that was not the case. So when the team loaded onto the bus from their Boston hotel, he joined his teammates.

"As we were busing to the rink from the hotel, right around Fenway, all you could see was people wearing [Flyers'] orange and [Bruins'] yellow," Syvret recalled. "Our bus was barely squeaking through the crowd; there were so many people. Our bus had tinted windows, so I don't think the fans could see through at us, but Flyers fans were all cheering and giving us thumbs up, while the Boston fans were giving us the finger and yelling at us."

Syvret was a junior star with the London Knights for three years, captaining the team to the Memorial Cup championship in 2004–05, the year NHL players were locked out. A solid five-foot-eleven, 205-pounder, Syvret put up great numbers in junior, including 23 goals and 69 points in his final season, and was named best defenceman in the Canadian Hockey League. Still, in his first few years of pro, he was not able to score as easily. In his first three season as a pro, Syvret played 28 games in the NHL—26 with the Edmonton Oilers and two with the Flyers. He managed just a single assist in those games.

"The Edmonton stints were so short that you can't really get yourself into a groove," he said. "I never really felt comfortable. I was called up at the end of the year, when Edmonton lost twenty-two games in a row, so all I was really concentrating on was trying not to get scored on. Once I got to Philly, I started to feel more comfortable and I was able to play my game. I had some scoring chances, but nothing was going in for me. Again, though, I was in and out of the lineup, and I'm at my best when I'm playing with confidence. When you are in and out of the lineup, you're afraid to take a chance rushing the puck in case you get caught. You know you might not play again."

By the time the Outdoor Classic rolled around, Syvret was confident in his ability to play at the NHL, and now it was simply a matter of producing enough that his coach, Peter Laviolette, and general manager, Paul Holmgren, would share his confidence. And what better time to score than in the outdoor game, with the eyes of the entire hockey world on him?

It turned out to be a day to remember for the twenty-five-year-old.

"It was pretty sweet," he said. "It was unbelievable. I don't know what it's like in other ballparks, but at Fenway, you walk from the locker room down a whole flight of stairs and under the concourse of the building, and then up more stairs into the dugout, and then you make the long trek to the ice surface. It was pretty insane. It was the loudest I'd ever heard a building, let alone an open building. There was a little bit of snow falling, so it was a pretty cool atmosphere.

"The day before the game, we had a practice, and it was unreal. It was snowing and everyone was happy and smiling on the ice because it felt like you were back to the days when you were a kid, playing outdoors at Christmastime back home in Ontario. To have my family there was special."

After a scoreless first period, during which the hometown Bruins outshot the visiting Flyers 9–6 on a gloriously sunny afternoon, Syvret became the first NHLer ever to notch his first big-league goal on a baseball diamond. And what a weird goal it was!

The play started with Flyers power forward Scott Hartnell skating close to the Bruins net and kicking the legs out from under Boston goaltender Tim Thomas, causing him to go sprawling to the ice. When Thomas got back to his feet, he was more focused on retribution than stopping pucks. So when a loose puck found its way to Syvret standing just inside the blue line, Thomas wasn't even looking in his direction. Instead, the Bruins stopper lunged out of his net to hit Hartnell. Although he was actually standing at the point with his back to the Boston net, Syvret wheeled around and fired the puck in one motion. It went through a maze of players and found the back of the Bruins net.

"Obviously, when I scored I was happy, but I was rattled at first because, just prior to that, we came down on a rush, and when Hartnell took out Thomas's feet, the puck had come off the boards and I was moving in to take a one-timer," Syvret said. "Their centre, Marc Savard, was coming toward me, and the only thing going through my mind was, 'Don't let him block your shot.' I was down so low that if he had blocked it, chances are the Bruins would have had a three-on-one. I didn't even look at the net. I was looking at Savard and knew I had to shoot the puck by him. I had the whole top of the net to shoot at, but I was more concerned with not having the shot blocked. The rebound from that shot came out to me, and I had a fadeaway shot that went in."

It's funny what goes through a player's mind in the heat of the action. On the play that resulted in Syvret's first NHL goal, he nearly passed on the opportunity to shoot.

"As I got to the puck, I was thinking of dishing it to our winger, Jeff Carter, who was open, because I didn't think my odds of scoring with my back to the net were very good," he said with a laugh. "I turned and hesitated for a split second, but by then I had run out of options, so I just fired it through someone's legs and that was all I saw. There was so much traffic in front I couldn't see the puck, but I did hear it hit the padding at the back of the net. I heard a *poof*!"

With his parents, brother, and uncle sitting in the stands, and many of his friends watching the game on TV, Syvret finally had his goal.

"Two days later, we played Toronto at home and I scored a much prettier goal, but getting that first one was amazing and a big relief," he said. "I was feeling on top of the world with two goals in three games. Two games later, I hurt my shoulder and I was done for the rest of the year."

He was done for the year, but came away with one amazing memory.

"I would have loved to have scored my first NHL goal at Maple Leaf Gardens, but to be honest, I wouldn't trade scoring my first NHL goal at Fenway Park for anything," Syvret said.

BILLY CARROLL

FEBRUARY 25, 1981

WINNING THE STANLEY CUP was a way of life for Billy Carroll. After all, although Carroll only played in the National Hockey League for seven seasons, the talented two-way centre won the Cup in four of his first five years in the league—three with the New York Islanders and the fourth with the Edmonton Oilers. Aside from the obvious, achieving the ultimate dream, Carroll said there were other benefits.

"Half of your money back in those days was made in bonuses, so you certainly start to think of that early in your career," Carroll said. "You'd earn around $5,000 per round. The first year we won the Cup, we earned an addition $28,000 in playoff bonuses, and the team matched that. My salary was $55,000 that season, and I earned an additional $58,000 in bonuses."

Carroll had been a scoring star for three years with the London Knights of the Ontario Hockey League, but when he turned pro in 1979, the Islanders' second-round pick, thirty-eighth overall, had different plans for him. The team already had enough players who knew how to fill the net with pucks.

"I was called to the coach's office before I even stepped on the ice [and met] with the coach, Al Arbour, GM Bill Torrey and chief scout Jim Devellano, and they told me I was going to go down to the minors and learn how to check, take faceoffs, and kill penalties," Carroll said. "When you look at the lineup they had, with Bryan Trottier, Butch Goring, and Bob Bourne at centre, the only way to really make that team for me was to do that. I actually enjoyed the role and had a lot of fun with it."

In fact, Carroll spent his first full year of pro playing in the minors with the Indianapolis Checkers of the Central Hockey League, where he scored 9 goals and 26 points in 49 games and learned to play more of a shutdown game. Carroll said the year in the CHL was huge in terms of overall development as a player.

"I believe after having done it, as long as you can stay healthy, it can add a lot of years to your career if you go down there and play in the minors before going to the NHL," he said. "The first big difference is you're playing with men. In junior, a lot of the bigger guys are a little bit slower. In pro, the big guys can move as well. The other thing was, everybody was at a higher level than what they were in junior.

"I had no choice. I had to learn which side of the shoulder to be on when checking an opponent on the puck, because I wasn't that big. It was all kinds of little things. From a positioning perspective, I had to learn how to play the angles."

Carroll's apprenticeship in the minors continued through most of his second pro season. This time, though, he better combined his ability to score, managing 27 goals and 64 points in 59 games, while he continued to improve on the defensive side of the puck. He was thrilled near the end of the season when he got the call from the Islanders.

"Hector Marini and I got called up to the Islanders and wound up staying the rest of the year," Carroll said. "There were injuries at the time that we came up, and then they made a couple of trades and different people got hurt again.

Every time we got close to being sent back, something would happen and we made it through the trade deadline and to the end of the year."

It was the start of a magical run for Carroll. He'll never forget his first NHL goal, although he can't be blamed for trying to erase the memory of the result from his mind. It was in an 11–4 loss to the Calgary Flames on February 25, 1981.

"It was in Calgary against Pat Riggin, my old goalie from junior," Carroll said. "I scored on a snap shot that went over his glove on a screened play. I don't think he even saw the puck. I rub it in every time I see him. He keeps telling me I wasn't the only one who scored on him.

"It was obviously a big deal for me, especially being in that old Calgary rink, the Corral. To me, getting my first shift in the NHL was an even bigger deal than actually scoring my first NHL goal. Once you get out there you're fine, but beforehand you are very nervous. Arbour was really good to Hector and me, getting us out early in the game so we didn't have to sit there too long worrying."

Carroll played the final eighteen games of the season with the Islanders and then dressed for all eighteen of the team's post-season games on the run to the Cup. He wound up with 4 goals and 8 points in the regular season and managed an impressive 3 goals and 12 points in the playoffs.

"I remember the first Stanley Cup victory and how long a run it is to win four series," Carroll said. "We played Minnesota in the final, and won that series in five games. The guys that were the key hockey players on our team in the playoffs were our best players every night. It was really something to watch."

Carroll became an Islander regular the next three years, the first two of which the Islanders won the Cup. While his point production wasn't what it had been in the past, he was a valuable and appreciated defensive centre who took pride in his play.

"I certainly did take satisfaction in my role," Carroll said. "Some nights, depending on the game, we didn't get a whole heck of a lot of ice, and you had to be ready when you were called upon; and then, other nights, depending on how many penalties we took, we played more than the guys on the power play did. Al was very good that way—he stuck to his guns and had a game plan. I was just very fortunate to be part of that side of the puck and not somewhere in the middle, not on the power play or the penalty killing.

"I just considered myself fortunate to be there. After being in the minors and seeing how good the players were down there, you really have to be lucky. The third and fourth lines in the NHL can go down and the top line in the minors can come up and you really don't notice a big difference. So I appreciated being there."

After a few years, the Islanders seemed to lose their appreciation for Carroll, and he was chosen by the Edmonton Oilers in the league's annual waiver draft on October 9, 1984. Carroll went from playing with two of the best scorers in the NHL at that time, Mike Bossy and Bryan Trottier, to hooking up with two of the best players of all time, Wayne Gretzky and Mark Messier. It was a return to Canada, where hockey is an obsession, and a distinct change in playing style.

"It was actually like night and day," Carroll said. "On the Islanders, we were all married and our coach, Al Arbour, was a an army general and ran it that way, while on the Oilers, most of the guys were single and our coach, Glen Sather, ran a much looser team. It was interesting for me to see two sides on how teams can be successful."

Getting the opportunity to play with Gretzky offered unexpected benefits.

"The first day I arrived in Edmonton, Wayne Gretzky gave me a car to use," Carroll said. "He called me up and said he had a spare Mercedes sitting around, so he lent it to me for the year. Tough luck, eh?"

Carroll played parts of two seasons with Edmonton and capped his career playing parts of two years with the Detroit Red Wings. However, injuries finally got the better of him and he retired following the 1986–87 season. His professional career wasn't as long as he'd hoped for, but it certainly was prosperous. Carroll is still the only player to win Cups for both the Islanders and Oilers.

Looking back, Carroll said he really isn't amazed that he won the Stanley Cup in four of his first five years in the NHL.

"When I look at the team photos and see who was on those teams, it really shouldn't be a surprise to anybody," Carroll said. "Look at the Hall of Famers that played on both teams. When I think about the team we had in Edmonton, if it wasn't for free agency and Gretzky moving when [owner] Peter Pocklington had money trouble, that team could have won ten Cups."

FRED PERLINI

FRED PERLINI WAS NEVER DUBBED the Can't Miss Kid, but when the strapping centreman put up 5 points in 7 NHL games as an underage pro, you had to think he was well on his way to a long and fruitful professional career. And he was . . . just not in the NHL.

Despite his unexpected heroics with the Toronto Maple Leafs in 1981–82, when he was summoned to play in the NHL from the Ontario Hockey League's Toronto Marlboros, Perlini appeared in just one NHL game after turning pro. Five points in seven games as a nineteen-year-old, and barely a sniff afterwards. Amazing!

"I think about it a lot," Perlini said. "It's not like I thought I had it made just because I had success when I was called up as a junior, but I must admit, I thought I was on the right path."

Who wouldn't? Perlini joined the Marlies as a seventeen-year-old in 1978–79, and the following season was drafted by the Maple Leafs in the eighth round, 158th overall.

In those days, it wasn't uncommon for NHL teams to summon players from the junior ranks when they were short-staffed. If their minor pro affiliate was located far away, while a player they had drafted was playing junior nearby, it just made sense. That was especially so for Toronto, since they shared Maple Leaf Gardens with the junior Marlies, while their farm team was in Moncton, New Brunswick. Although Perlini had not signed with the Leafs, he could play with them on an amateur tryout.

"The first time I got called up was December 30, against St. Louis," Perlini said. "Laurie Boschman was injured for the Leafs. I'll never forget—I was on the ice with the Marlies. and I got a phone call that went through our trainer, Dave Marr. He came up to me and said, 'Fred, you're playing for the Leafs tonight.'

"I was kind of shocked. I didn't even have a suit. I had a pair of jeans and a shirt, and my roommate, Jim Malone, went to our house and got me a suit so I could at least walk out of the rink after the game with a suit on. I virtually went from one side of the rink to the other. It happened so fast, my head was spinning. My heart was pounding. I was excited, but scared to death. It happened so fast, I think that was the best way for it to happen. It didn't give me too much time to worry about what was happening."

A lot of kids would have been starstruck, but Perlini had an advantage.

"I knew all the guys from training camp," he said. "Guys like Darryl Sittler and Borje Salming were amazing. When I got into the dressing room, they made me feel right at home. It helped ease the shock of being called up right out of the blue. They used to give us sticks all the time after practice. They really looked after the Marlie players. It was a thrill for us to use their sticks.

"The first thing I did when I got to the dressing room was call home to tell my family I was going to play in the NHL. I think they got to listen to it on the radio. The Leafs didn't get the coverage that they do these days."

Perlini was pleased with his NHL debut, although he didn't score a goal.

"The night went okay," he said. "I used to play the point on the power play in junior, and the coach, Mike Nykolyuk, sent me out to play the point on the power play with Salming. I was shocked. It was like, 'Are you kidding me?' The first game goes well. I got a regular shift playing centre on the fourth line and actually got an assist in the game. They were flying out to Detroit right after the game, and they said, 'Fred, you're in the lineup tomorrow against the Red Wings. You're flying out with us.' I grew up [in Sault Ste. Marie, Ontario] a Red Wings fan, so I was thrilled."

After spending the night in a Detroit hotel with veteran defenceman Jim Korn as his roommate, Perlini set out to play his favourite team.

"Again, everything happened so fast," Perlini said. "As well as I thought played in my first game, my second game was better. I scored a goal and an assist and I was named the second star. My goal was a power-play goal that was assisted by Sittler and Wilf Paiment. Sittler took a shot and I busted into the slot for the rebound, and then I top-shelfed it. Sittler was breaking in from the left side, and I was cutting right through the slot. The puck came to me and I rifled it home. It was a read-and-react [play], and I just rifled it."

Perlini was called up a few more times and said he felt right at home playing in the NHL. In fact, one day he played for the Marlies in the afternoon and scored a hat trick against the Niagara Falls Flyers, was summoned by the Leafs that night, and scored his second NHL goal against fellow Soo native Tony Esposito of the Chicago Blackhawks.

"I must admit, where I was at with my head, I'm not really sure, but I was pretty confident with my game at the time," he said. "Even though I was a junior, I was putting up a lot of points with the Marlies and I was very confident with my skill and ability at the time.

"After I went back to the Marlies, [agent] Bill Watters said the Leafs were interested in signing me, but he said, 'There's no way you're signing an eighth-round contract!' From what I was told at the time, I ended up signing a second-round contract. I didn't get the big signing bonus, but it was a decent bonus.

"Coming home that year, I was very, very proud. I was so proud to be a Leaf and to have played in the NHL."

Perlini graduated from junior after the 1981–82 season and spent the next four years playing in the AHL. He was called up by the Leafs once, in 1983–84, but that was it. He put up decent numbers in the minors, but it didn't help his cause. He couldn't understand how he could enjoy such amazing success as a nineteen-year-old and not get the chance to show what he could do in the NHL over an extended period of time.

"You scratch your head and you start losing confidence," Perlini said. "You lose faith in yourself. All these good hockey players who were great juniors were playing with me in the American league, as well as lots of veterans. I was told over and over, 'Don't worry, kid; you'll get your shot.' But I never got back up again. I just wanted to wear the jersey and play in the NHL. I was a kid from up north who just loved to play hockey.

"I'd go home to the Soo in the summer, and people would say, 'They don't like Italians'—crazy things like that which I never believed. I always thought, for the amount of time the Leafs gave me, I produced. If they needed me to work on things, they never really told me what exactly they were.

There was never any feedback. I work with kids now, and the feedback is incredible. They know what they have to work on. With the Maple Leafs, it was just a revolving door."

Eventually, Perlini joined the New York Rangers organization, but once again he was ticketed for the minors. That's when he gave up the NHL dream and headed for Europe—England, to be exact.

"I was making five, six hundred dollars a week," Perlini said. "To me it wasn't real hockey. It was okay . . . competitive, but not what I was used to. The next thing I know, former NHLer Al Sims, who was coaching in Scotland, a team in Fife, calls and asks me to join him. They were paying good money. I was still hoping to play in Italy at that point, but Al said I had to at least come up and take a look around.

"It was about a half-hour from St. Andrews [the Royal & Ancient Golf Club] and the money they were paying was unreal—about $60,000 tax free. They also gave us 10 per cent of the gate in three chunks of the gate money during the season. Al used to sit on the bench, and we'd be winning the game, and he'd be wiping his visor and he'd. say, 'Hey guys, another full house tonight!' We'd crack up on the bench."

The hockey wasn't great, and Perlini moved from team to team before finally settling into playing with the Guildford Flames the final three years of his playing career. The hockey was mediocre, but he loved living in England.

"I ended up settling in Guildford," Perlini said. "We settled as a family. There was a guy who was the CEO of Morgan Stanley, John Hepburn, who started the professional team from scratch. I played my last three years for him, but I told him, 'John, I've been bouncing around from team to team and I don't want to do this anymore.'

"He said, 'You play your last three or four years here and then you run the program,' and that's exactly what I did. I was in charge of the whole junior program. I brought in the coaches and made more in that job than I ever did as a player."

Ultimately, Perlini enjoyed a fruitful professional hockey career that many others only dream about. And even though his initial foray into the National Hockey League didn't lead to a long career in that league, he can still say he scored in the best league in the world.

DOUG BROWN

OCTOBER 9, 1987

MOST PLAYERS CHERISH THE PUCK they shot to score their first NHL goal. You see them dive into the net to retrieve it as if it were a winning lottery ticket, and just looking at it years later causes a flood of timeless memories to take over their very being.

Doug Brown is not most players.

Sure, he got the puck after scoring his first NHL goal for the New Jersey Devils on October 9, 1987. Nothing strange about that. But over the years, Brown lost track of the puck. He knew it was kicking around the house somewhere, but if you asked to see it, it might take an hour or two to find.

So imagine Doug Brown's colossal surprise as he made his way up the driveway to his home one day and tried to make his way past his two children—Patrick, five, and Anna, six—who were deeply engrossed in a friendly game of street hockey. As Brown avoided the commotion, he noticed something vaguely familiar about the puck they were battering around.

Wait a minute . . . isn't that—

Indeed it was. Patrick and Anna were horsing around using the puck he had tucked away in a box.

"After I scored my first NHL goal, the Devils' trainers were able to put a piece of tape on the puck, and put the date as well as DOUG BROWN'S 1ST NHL GOAL AGAINST PITTSBURGH," said Brown. "But you know what happens over time . . . you move around from house to house and you lose track of it. You know it's there, and you'd certainly never lose it, but you might not be able to put your hands on it without a little search of the house."

Brown, a native of Southborough, Massachusetts, wasn't a natural goal scorer, but he was no stranger to the net, either. In his third year at Boston College, he led the Eagles with 37 goals in 45 games and was second on the team in points, with 68. He was signed as a free agent by the Devils, and in his first year of pro, Brown scored 24 goals and 58 points in 73 games with the Maine Mariners of the American Hockey league.

Yet, when the five-foot-ten, 195-pound right winger finally found his way to the NHL in 1986–87, it wasn't scoring the Devils wanted from him.

"It was at about the 60-game point of the NHL season," Brown recalled. "The Devils had four games coming up, starting with two against the Islanders, and then games against Edmonton and Winnipeg. Doug Carpenter was the coach of the Devils at the time and he pulled me aside and said, 'I'd like you to check the other team's best scorer.' So in my first four NHL games, I had to try to shut down Mike Bossy, Mike Bossy again, Wayne Gretzky, and Dale Hawerchuk. That was my four-game introduction to the NHL. Welcome to the NHL!"

Brown doesn't recall having a good chance to score his first NHL goal during that four-game stretch while trying to shut down three Hall of Famers.

However, the following season, when he finally made the Devils as a regular, he struck for 14 goals and 25 points in 70 games and then managed an impressive 5 goals and 6 points in 19 playoff games.

Brown's first NHL goal was a shorthanded tally that occurred very quickly after he managed to outfox yet another future Hall of Famer, Mario Lemieux. Five years later, Brown and Lemieux were teammates with the Penguins, but on this night they were trying to outdo one another.

"It was the result of a turnover in the neutral zone," Brown said. "It was just the two of us in the neutral zone, and he was back by his own blue line in a regroup situation. He didn't have any support, being the last man back, and he tried to look me off and throw a back diagonal pass, which I was able to read. It doesn't happen often, but I was able to read that one and intercept his pass."

Brown quickly looked up and, yes indeed, found himself on a breakaway. Finally, his moment of truth.

"The whole thing first was trying to play cat-and-mouse with Mario, which is not an easy thing for any player to do, and the next thing was realizing I was in alone on Pat Riggin, a pretty good goaltender," Brown said. "I was trying to size him up as I moved in. Was he ready for a shot, or was he ready for a deke? You have to do the opposite. He was pretty far out of his net, so I decided I would try to deke him. I faked a shot and went to my forehand."

Brown couldn't believe it as he saw the puck cross the goal line.

"You have that adrenaline rush," Brown said. "You've scored thousands of goals growing up, and you want to prove you can do it at every level. To be honest, every time you score a goal in the NHL, whether it's your first goal or second goal or 100th or, for the superstars, their 1,000th goal, you still have that adrenaline rush . . . you grow six inches every time you score a goal. It's a rush. All of a sudden you feel like you are six foot six and 250 pounds and you are Superman."

Ultimately, Brown developed into a solid two-way performer in the NHL, a valued third-liner who could pop the occasional goal, but was at his best as a checker. He scored 160 goals and 376 points in 854 games with the Devils, Penguins, and Detroit Red Wings, whom he helped win Stanley Cups in 1996–97 and 1997–98. The Red Wings so valued his consistent play that, when Brown was claimed by the Nashville Predators in the 1998 expansion draft, Detroit immediately traded to reacquire him, giving up Petr Sykora and two draft picks.

So, what ultimately became of the puck Patrick and Anna were playing with in the driveway?

"To be honest, I'm not sure," Brown said. "I know it's around somewhere."

SEVEN

HALL OF FAMERS

Previous page: Mike Bossy of the New York Islanders celebrates a goal against the Vancouver Canucks en route to winning the 1982 Stanley Cup. (Getty Images)

BRETT HULL

IN MAY OF 1986, WHEN THE third-youngest son of hockey legend Bobby Hull skated onto the ice with the visiting Calgary Flames before a playoff game at the famous Montreal Forum, his famous bloodline couldn't stop his knees from knocking or ease the deafness that filled his ears. At that moment, he was just like any other kid making his NHL debut.

"That was actually pretty scary," Brett Hull recalled. "I don't think I was prepared mentally or physically for the NHL at that time."

And yet, there he was in Montreal, just twenty-one years old and with his Flames' series with the Canadiens tied 1–1. Fresh off an impressive 54-goal and 84-point season with the University of Minnesota Duluth, Hull certainly had aspirations to follow in his dad's footsteps and play in the NHL, but with his career suddenly fast-tracked, he felt a little out of place.

"I knew I wanted to turn pro, but our season in Duluth had ended before the NCAA playoffs had even started," Hull says. "I was still a college kid, and I wasn't expecting to be signed by the Flames until after the NHL season ended. I figured I'd be able to start working out in the summer and go to training camp as a fresh new face in the Calgary organization. All of a sudden, after two months off, I sign a contract with the Flames while they are just getting going in the playoffs.

I wasn't prepared for what I was about to go through, but it was a great experience and it gave me a pretty good idea about what it was going to take to be successful in the NHL."

Still, the professional career of one of hockey's greatest goal scorers was born, even if a little prematurely. If you saw Hull play then, you can be forgiven for thinking there's no way he would come close to matching his father's status in the sport. Hull wasn't a particularly adept skater, and physical conditioning, his father's calling card, was not high on his list of priorities.

Brett, admittedly, was never really into conditioning. He was a happy-go-lucky kid who lived life day by day with a satisfied grin on his face. Unlike his brothers, Blake and Bobby Jr., who followed in their father's footsteps and played junior hockey with the Cornwall Royals (Bobby Sr. was a junior star with the St. Catharines Teepees), Brett elected to play U.S. college hockey at the University of Minnesota Duluth. It was a great way for the son of a legend to stay out of the spotlight.

But there was one thing Brett shared with Bobby Hull: a great shot. Get Bobby the puck in a good shooting position, and there was a very good chance you'd add to your assist total. Ditto for Brett. His goal was to make himself invisible on the ice and then pop up for a scoring opportunity.

In 100 games over two NCAA seasons with the Bulldogs, Hull scored 84 goals and 144 points. At first blush it might seem unusual that Hull lasted until the 117th pick in the 1984 NHL entry draft. How could a future Hall of Famer be ignored for so long? Simple. He was eligible for the 1982 draft, but at the time he was playing juvenile hockey and was not on the NHL radar. The next year he played Tier II, and played well, but he still was not considered a prospect because there were questions about his commitment to the game...as well as his upside. In retrospect, it may be more shocking that he was picked as high as 117th! Back then if a team drafted a player, it didn't lose the player's rights if it failed to sign him. The Flames probably figured he's the son of the Golden Jet so what the heck.

Though Brett didn't score in the two games he played with the Flames in the 1985–86 Stanley Cup playoffs, he sure came close.

"Oh my god, I had so many scoring chances in those two games," Hull says. "I hit the post on my first shot . . . in my first shift . . . in my first game in the Montreal Forum . . . in the Stanley Cup final. I will never forget that moment. So close! I had multiple scoring chances, and just like a young kid who was not so sure of his surroundings, I couldn't bury them."

Hull wound up with one shot on goal in his NHL debut and was also along for the ride when Calgary was shut out 1–0 in game four. He sat out the fifth and deciding game of the series.

The following September, Hull arrived in Calgary for his first full pro season, but even with two playoff games under his belt, the Flames felt he needed more seasoning and assigned him to the Moncton Golden Flames of the American Hockey League. It proved to be a very good decision, as Hull took his game to the next level, scoring 50 goals and 92 points in 67 games and being named the AHL's rookie of the year.

Midway through the campaign, the Flames summoned Hull again, and this time he didn't let them down.

"I don't think I forget any of my goals," Hull says, "but I certainly remember my first. We were playing Hartford, and the game was tied in the third period. I was out there with another young guy, Gary Roberts. We were on a rush, and I cut through the middle and he threw a pass that got up in the air. I reached up and grabbed it with my glove, and then set it down on the ice. I went in on a breakaway on Steve Weeks and fired one on his blocker side over his right pad. It ended up being the game-winner in my first official NHL [regular-season] game, so I was pretty excited."

And thus, the Golden Brett was born.

Brett's dad, Bobby Hull, had the body of a Greek god. He was the poster child for fit professional athletes. In fact, one of the most famous pictures of the Golden Jet was taken of a shirtless Hull, in his early twenties, pitching hay back home on the farm in Belleville, Ontario, during the off-season. With his blonde curls and ripples, he looks more like a Hollywood movie star than a hockey player.

Once he turned pro, Brett Hull rapidly developed into one of the best snipers in NHL history. In just his second full season in the NHL, he scored 41 goals with the St. Louis Blues, and then, over the next three years, he pumped more rubber past NHL goaltenders than any player over a three-year span with seasons of 72, 86, and 70 goals.

All told, Hull scored 741 goals (131 more than his dad) and 650 assists for 1,391 points, and was the first son of an NHL 50-goal scorer to score 50 goals himself. He established an NHL record for most goals in a season by a right winger (86, in 1990–91), and helped the Dallas Stars and Detroit Red Wings win the Stanley Cup, in 1999 and 2002 respectively.

Hull's Stanley Cup–winning goal in 1999 against the Buffalo Sabres remains one of the most controversial in NHL history. The league had adopted a zero-tolerance policy for players scoring with a foot in the goal crease that season, but when Hull tallied at 14:51 of the third overtime period and players, team personnel, and the media instantly stormed the ice, the NHL quickly fudged the rule to say that a player could indeed score as long as the puck had entered the crease first.

In the end, Brett Hull was his own man. He broke free from his father's shadow and became a superstar in his own right.

"The pressure was there, but my personality and life experiences, growing up watching my two older bothers trying to do what they did, gave me a good learning curve on how to not be Bobby Hull's son," Brett says. "I figured out early I'd better decide who Brett Hull is. Once I did that, it became easy, because there was nothing in me mentally saying, 'Bobby Hull . . . Bobby Hull . . .' I am Brett Hull, and I could just go out and do my own thing."

MIKE BOSSY

OCTOBER 13, 1977

YOU WOULD THINK AFTER WATCHING Mike Bossy light up NHL goaltenders like they were backup peewee stoppers that NHL scouts would have changed their minds about how they viewed potential scoring stars from the Quebec Major Junior Hockey League. But Bossy isn't so sure.

Back when he was drafted fifteenth overall by the New York Islanders in 1977 (and forty-fourth overall by the Indianapolis Racers of the WHA), after scoring an incredible 309 goals in four seasons in the QMJHL, players from his junior league were considered "soft" by NHL teams. The Western Hockey League, with its long, gruelling bus trips, supposedly supplied the NHL with "tough" players.

"That's exactly how it was," Bossy said. "I don't really know if it has changed that much in terms of the classification of players. Back then, it was the big, tough, character guys came from the west; the all-around players, both offence and defence, came from Ontario; and the less character, scoring guys came from the east. I think if you talk with people who don't mind saying it the way it is, that's probably how it is still classified today."

Despite putting up awe-inspiring numbers with the Laval Titan, the slick-skating Bossy wasn't as highly regarded as one might expect come draft day. Some scouts questioned his courage, although the prejudice against players from the QMJHL probably played a huge role that opinion. This was the year that Dale McCourt of the St. Catharines Fincups was all the rage, though if truth be told, McCourt came nowhere close to matching Bossy's prowess as a professional hockey player. For that matter, nor did any of the fourteen players who were selected ahead of Bossy, although some, including Barry Beck, Doug Wilson, Lucien DeBlois, and Mark Napier, carved out pretty good careers for themselves.

Exactly what the Toronto Maple Leafs were thinking when they chose Trevor Johansen with the twelfth-overall pick ahead of Bossy, well, we'll never know. Even the Islanders had some doubts about Bossy. When it was their turn to pick, it came down to Bossy and another player who was considerably tougher, but much less skilled. They elected to go with the goal scorer.

Although Bossy made the Islanders straight out of junior, there were a few bumps along the road.

"I didn't have a particularly good training camp, and I had a couple of injuries," Bossy recalled. "I hurt my shoulder, and when I went to the doctor, he said there was a pre-existing condition and that if it happened again, I would have to have surgery. I was like, 'You've got to be kidding.' Then, in practice, there was a deflection and the puck hit me in the eye, so back I went to the doctor. I remember Bryan [Trottier] saying, 'This guy is our first-round pick and every time I see him he's in the infirmary.'

"I would phone my wife every day, and toward the end of training camp I told her I might have to start off playing in the minor leagues. She asked me where the Islanders' farm team was, and I told her Fort Worth.

"'Where is that?' she said.

"'In Texas.'

"She paused and said, 'Good luck.'

If there were any doubts about Bossy's potential, they were erased in his first NHL game, when he scored. The Islanders lost the game 3–2, but Bossy was well on his way to becoming one of the most prolific goal scorers in NHL history. It helped matters that he was placed on a line with two other rising stars, namely Trottier and rugged left winger Clark Gillies. Nobody knew it then, of course, but all three would wind up in the Hockey Hall of Fame.

"I remember two things distinctly from my first game, which was against the Buffalo Sabres," Bossy said. "One is that I drove to the net and got a rebound and popped a backhand shot in for my first goal. Don Edwards was in net for the Sabres. The other thing is, I was a pretty even-keeled guy, so when we were getting ready before the game, I looked over at Bryan and said, 'I'm going to treat this just like any other exhibition game.' He looked me straight in the eye and said, 'This is no exhibition game.'"

That was an illustration of exactly how intense Trottier was. Bossy, meanwhile, proved all those who thought he was either too soft or couldn't skate well enough—or both— wrong. The funny thing is, Bossy said he really didn't have to change anything about his game to make the adjustment to the NHL. It was business as usual.

"There really wasn't much of a transition for me," Bossy said. "I think I scored 20 goals in my first 25 games."

That's not to suggest it was all peaches and cream.

"The first sort of stumbling block for me came in our first game in Detroit in the Olympia, our twenty-third game of the year," Bossy said. "We go out for the opening faceoff, and lined up across from us are Dennis Polonich, Dennis Hextall, and Dan Maloney—their three tough guys. As soon as the puck was dropped, all the gloves were on the ice, and it was a five-on-five brawl. That was my 'Welcome to the NHL' moment. Maloney didn't land any punches, but he tossed me around like a rag doll."

Bossy completed his freshman season with an amazing 53 goals, an NHL record for rookies at the time, and 91 points in 73 games and was named the NHL's rookie of the year. If he didn't make believers out of those who had doubted him in his first year, he surely did when he followed it up with 69 goals and 126 points in 80 games as a sophomore. In fact, Bossy not only scored 50 goals or more in each of his first nine NHL seasons, he actually scored 60 or more in six of those years.

During the 1980–81 campaign, Bossy was the second player—after Maurice "Rocket" Richard—to score 50 goals in 50 NHL games. Richard had done it in 1944–45, thirty-six years earlier. In a wonderful gesture, Richard sent Bossy a telegram of congratulations following the game in which he matched the Rocket's feat.

In Bossy's third season, the Islanders won their first of four consecutive Stanley Cups. During the 1980–81 playoffs, in the Islanders' third straight championship year, Bossy scored a whopping 17 goals and 35 points in 18 games and was named winner of the Conn Smythe Trophy as most valuable player in the post-season. He scored 17 goals in the playoffs in three consecutive seasons.

Bossy's career was cut short because of back problems, but even in his tenth and final season, when he played injured most nights, he still managed 38 goals and 75 points in 63 games. All told, Bossy scored 573 goals and 1,126 points in 752 regular-season games and added 85 goals and 160 points in 129 playoff games. He won the Lady Byng Trophy as the NHL's most gentlemanly player three times, finishing his career with just 210 penalty minutes.

Wayne Gretzky, considered by many to be the greatest player who ever played in the NHL, was once asked who he thought was the best right winger of all time. Without hesitation, the Great One responded: "Mike Bossy." When you consider that Gordie Howe, Rocket Richard, Bernie Geoffrion, Guy Lafleur, and Jaromir Jagr also played right wing, that's mighty high praise.

TEEMU SELANNE

MOST PLAYERS ARRIVE AT THEIR FIRST NHL training camp prepared to play games. Not Teemu Selanne. The eighteen-year-old Finn, who is destined to be named to the Hall of Fame, was under the assumption that the Winnipeg Jets had brought him in simply to let him train with pros; to acclimatize him to the North American lifestyle and NHL players.

"My first game against the Minnesota North Stars was nerve-racking," Selanne said. "I had no idea that I was going to get into an exhibition game. I was in the Finnish army at the time, which is mandatory, and I knew I had to go back home to the army. I figured I was just there for two weeks to get a little taste of what the NHL was like, and then I'd go back home to play in the Finnish league. One day, our general manager, John Ferguson, came up to me and said, 'You're playing tonight.' I said, 'What?' I was so nervous it was almost like being in shock. But it was fun. I played on a line with Dale Hawerchuk and Brent Ashton, and it was great."

It was a lasting memory, indeed, but Selanne wouldn't make it to the NHL as a full-time player until a couple of years later. Unlike a lot of youngsters, Selanne had the benefit of first playing professionally against men back home with Jokerit in the first division of the Finnish league. So, by the time Winnipeg's first-round pick, tenth overall, from the 1988 entry draft cracked the roster, he had valuable experience. In fact, you could make the case that few players arrived in the NHL as ready for instant stardom as the six-foot, 196-pound right winger. Even so, Selanne took nothing for granted.

"Of course you are little bit nervous," Selanne said. "I come from Finland, and the NHL game is so different because of the smaller ice surface in the NHL. There were a lot of questions in my mind about what I was up against. And there were a lot of things you need to adjust to as soon as possible. That said, I had confidence in myself, but you never know what kind of a chance you are going to get in your first year. I had signed a big contract, so I knew that was going to help me, but I didn't really know what to expect."

Neither did the hockey world. It didn't take long, however, for everyone to realize that somebody quite special had arrived—not that it should have been that big a surprise. Selanne had led the Finnish league in scoring the season before, as a twenty-one-year-old.

"Everything started clicking right away," Selanne said. "I was very pleased that I adjusted to all those new things quickly."

Selanne made his mark quickly, drawing two assists in his NHL debut, a 4–1 win over the Detroit Red Wings on October 6, 1992. Two nights later, Selanne scored the first of what would be a record-breaking 76 goals that season, and the Finnish Flash, as he became known, was born.

"I remember it like it was yesterday, because I scored my first NHL goal in the legendary old Cow Palace in [San Francisco]," Selanne said. "It was on the power play and, like a lot of my goals, it was a slapshot from the side. I remember Keith Tkachuk was standing in front of the net, setting a good screen so the goalie couldn't see. I remember thinking how good it felt to get that first one."

Fifteen years earlier, Mike Bossy of the New York Islanders had established the NHL record for most goals in a season by a rookie with 53. Selanne obliterated that mark, beating it by 23. In fact, Selanne let it be known to all that he was a player to be reckoned with when he scored 11 goals and 19 points in his first 11 NHL games, en route to being named the NHL's rookie of the year. Selanne had one four-goal game, four hat tricks, and 12 two-goal games that season. He wound up fifth in league scoring with 132 points in 84 games.

Selanne also became the first European to lead the NHL in goal scoring, tying Alexander Mogilny of the Buffalo Sabres that season. For Selanne, it was a dream come true.

"When I was young and growing up in Finland, the NHL was almost like a fantasy," he said. "There weren't very many Finnish players in the NHL. Obviously, Jari Kurri was the biggest star from Finland. When we realized he was having so much success in the NHL, he gave kids in Finland hope and belief that it you worked hard and got a little bit lucky, you can make the NHL. Nobody really knew how much work it would take or how you would even get to the NHL. What is the road to the NHL?"

Although Selanne would never come close to scoring 76 goals again in his career, he achieved a lot to be proud of, including helping the Anaheim Ducks win the Stanley Cup in 2006–07. He scored 40 or more goals five times in his career, and he is the first player in NHL history over the age of thirty-five to have back-to-back 40-goal seasons. Selanne was a first team NHL all-star twice and a second team all-star twice, was the most valuable player in the 1998 NHL All-Star Game, and won the Rocket Richard Trophy in 1999 for leading the league with 47 goals.

Although he temporarily retired after Anaheim's Cup victory, he returned to action midway through the following season and continued to play at a high level. Selanne looks back fondly on his first year in the NHL.

"I don't ever think I felt it was easy, but I couldn't believe how often I scored," he said. "First of all, the hockey was different back then. I would get at least two breakaways every game. I think the mindset back then was whoever could score the most goals would win. These days, it's almost the opposite. It's all about preventing goals and scoring situations. I was so hungry. If I scored one goal, I knew I needed another one. If I got the second goal, I really wanted the third one. It was just amazing.

"It all happened so fast, it was like being on a roller coaster. You didn't even have time to stop and think about what was going on. I don't think it was until the following season that I actually looked back and got a feel for what I went through.

"The thing is, everybody only has one chance to break the record," Selanne said. "I think it is going to be a very difficult record to break. Mike Bossy held the record before me and he held it for fifteen years. It is going to be hard, especially with how much hockey has changed."

There are few NHL records that are unbreakable. The one people mention most often is goaltender Glenn Hall's 502 consecutive starts over eight seasons. With the wear and tear players endure nowadays, that mark should be safe for all time. However, Selanne's rookie record of 76 goals might be just as secure.

LUC ROBITAILLE

WHAT'S BETTER THAN SCORING your first NHL goal? Try scoring your first NHL goal on your first shift and—here's the kicker—on a pass from your childhood hero.

In a city best known for its district of Hollywood, where they pay people big bucks to write this kind of a script, Luc Robitaille lived it for real. Robitaille, who grew up in Montreal idolizing Marcel Dionne, got the opportunity to play with—and live with—Dionne when he was a rookie for the Los Angeles Kings in 1986–87.

"I remember Marcel asked me as training camp was going on, 'If you make the team, what would you like to do?'" Robitaille said. "I said, 'If I make the team, I want to live with a family. I don't want to think about anything except playing hockey.'

"Marcel had been playing in Los Angeles at the time for ten years, and I was the first kid he had heard say that. Most of the kids who made the Kings would say, 'I want to go to Hollywood,' or 'I want to go to the beach.' It was funny— Jimmy Carson, who was just eighteen, Steve Duchesne, who was twenty-one, and myself, we all said the same thing. Marcel was so happy to hear that, and so excited, that he decided to help us. I lived in Marcel's house; Jimmy lived at his next-door neighbour's house; and Steve Duchesne was about a mile down the road from us, living with another family. That made the transition a lot easier for us."

Many wondered exactly what to expect from Robitaille when he turned pro. He had been a prolific scorer in junior, firing 155 goals and 424 points in just 197 games with the Hull Olympiques of the Quebec Major Junior Hockey League, but wasn't drafted until the ninth round, 171st overall, in 1984. Little did anybody know that Robitaille, along with fellow King Dave Taylor, would become the lowest-drafted players to achieve 1,000 points in their careers.

It didn't take long for people to appreciate the fact that, while his skating might not be as fluid as most NHLers, Robitaille had a nose for the net and spectacular hands. And what a thrill it was to get the chance to play with Dionne.

"Coming into my first training camp and seeing the way Marcel handled himself was so cool," Robitaille said. "He treated the young players so well. He really had a huge impact on me."

Robitaille didn't have to wait long for his first NHL goal, although if you ask him about it today, he'll tell you a different story.

"Our first game was at home against the St. Louis Blues, and Pat Quinn, our coach, decided to spread the scoring around a bit," Robitaille said. "Dave Taylor was going to play with Jimmy Carson and Marcel Dionne was going to play with me. The third line, or whatever you want to call it, had Bernie Nicholls, so we had three scoring lines.

"When the game started, he started Bernie's line and then went with Taylor's line. Then something happened and he went back to Nicholls' line, and I remember sitting on the bench, and suddenly it's been over four minutes from the start of the game and I'm going crazy because I haven't been on the ice yet. Marcel leaned over and said, 'Don't worry, our chance is coming, kid . . . It's coming, kid.' About thirty seconds later, Quinn called for our line to go next. The centres always changed first, so Marcel jumped over the boards. Then whoever was the left winger came to change, so I jumped on the ice. Someone dumped the puck in and the Blues' goalie, Rick Wamsley, went behind the net and played the puck to his left along the wall.

"I saw that Marcel anticipated it, and Wamsley didn't get good wood on the puck. Marcel was about at the hash mark when he corralled the puck. When I saw that, I hurried as fast as I could to the front of the net and yelled as loud as I could, 'Marcel! Marcel!' because the goalie wasn't there yet. Marcel saw me and passed it, and in one motion I tipped it into the empty net. That was my first shot and my first goal. I literally went from the bench to the front of the net and tipped the puck in for my first goal. It was the greatest feeling!

"Marcel was so happy. To Marcel, it was fun to see young guys have success; especially young guys who were really dedicated to the game, because that's the way he was."

Not only did Robitaille lead the Kings in scoring in his first year, with 45 goals and 84 points in 79 games, he was named the Calder Trophy winner as the NHL's rookie of the year. Through his nineteen-year career, during which he would also play with the Pittsburgh Penguins, Detroit Red Wings, and New York Rangers, Robitaille had three different stints with the Kings and led the team in scoring eight times. He was second in club scoring five times, including four times behind Wayne Gretzky.

Upon retiring following the 2005–06 season, Robitaille remained with the Kings organization as the president of business operations. Robitaille retired as the top goal-scoring

(668) and point-producing (1,394) left winger in NHL history. He played in eight NHL All-Star Games and was a member of the Red Wings' Stanley Cup championship team in 2001–02. He also helped Canada win a gold medal at the World Championship in 1994.

Robitaille was inducted into the Hockey Hall of Fame in 2009. He went into the Hall along with former Red Wings teammates Steve Yzerman and Brett Hull, as well as ex-New York Rangers teammate Brian Leetch.

Robitaille had the pleasure of playing with many of the game's biggest stars, including Gretzky, Mark Messier, Mario Lemieux, Brian Leetch, Rob Blake, Sergei Fedorov, Steve Yzerman, Nicklas Lidstrom, Chris Chelios, and Brett Hull.

"The funny thing I rarely got to play on those guys' lines," Robitaille said with a chuckle. "However, I did get to play on Marcel's line, and that was truly amazing."

Rogers Sportsnet

MIKE BROPHY is a hockey analyst for Rogers Sportsnet, a syndicated columnist and twice-weekly analyst for The Team 990 in Montreal. Brophy covered junior hockey for the *Peterborough Examiner* for 14 years and served as a senior writer with *The Hockey News* for 17 years. The Hamilton, Ontario, native has been writing about hockey for more than thirty years and has won six Ontario Newswire writing awards for his coverage of junior hockey. Brophy won the Benjamin Franklin Award for best new voice for his book *Curtis Joseph: The Acrobat.* He has collaborated with Ralph Mellanby, renowned executive television producer of *Hockey Night in Canada,* on two bestselling books: *The Legends of Hockey* and *Let the Games Begin.*

Brophy and his wife, Marilyn, live in Pickering, Ontario, and have three children, Chase, Blair, and Darryl.